Ukrainian Food Flair

Authentic Recipes from Canada's West Coast

Recipes and Stories by Sylvia Molnar

Edited by Paulette MacQuarrie

As heard on Nash Holos
Ukrainian Roots Radio

ISBN: 978-0-9810378-2-0

Contents

Nash Holos
Ukrainian Roots Radio
Наш Голос

Follow on your favorite platform!

 **NashHolos.com**

 **Amazon Music**

 **Spotify**

 **Apple Podcasts**

 **Facebook**

 **YouTube**

 **Acast RSS feed**

 **Patreon**

Introduction

Ukrainian Food Flair is both a long-running radio series and a cookbook that has been a long time coming.

The idea for the book started back in the early 2000s when Sylvia Molnar was still with us, and was presenting a delightful mix of recipes, cooking tips and personal anecdotes called "Ukrainian Food Flair" on Nash Holos Ukrainian Roots Radio in Vancouver, British Columbia.

When Sylvia told me of her dream to publish her recipes, it soon became my dream too! I loved the idea of getting the wonderful recipes and stories she presented on the show into print.

We spent many hours together planning and preparing, dreaming and scheming. But of course, it started with organizing all of Sylvia's recipes, tips and anecdotes that she shared on the show. A daunting task in itself!

Sylvia spent hours gathering all the hand-written scripts that she read on the air (fortunately she saved them!), and I spent countless hours typing them up—without the aid of modern digital assistance. Then we proofread, edited, re-wrote, and edited again. Finally, we were satisfied and felt ready to submit our cookbook manuscript to publishers.

After several disappointing rejections, we decided to take a stab at self-publishing. Back in the early 2000s, self-publishing was still new and presented quite a challenge. We made several attempts, but given our inexperience, we were unable to meet the challenge.

Eventually, Sylvia retired, and by 2010 we had each gone our separate ways. Sadly, in 2015 Sylvia passed away.

Because I had audio recordings of all of Sylvia's recipes, from time to time I would air them in her memory. Listeners of the Nanaimo edition of the show were particularly intrigued with the recipes and her stories. So from time to time, I thought about revisiting the cookbook project. But with Sylvia gone, I just wasn't inspired or motivated to get back to it. It was too sad of a reminder.

Then one day, Sylvia's sister Leone called me out of the blue. It was on January 6th, which was Ukrainian Christmas Eve to us "old timers" and certainly had been in Sylvia's day. It was always a special date even if we didn't celebrate it anymore with the typical lavish ritual feast.

Leone had recently come across Sylvia's copy of the cookbook manuscript and my phone number. So she called to ask if I might consider trying again to publish it as a tribute to Sylvia's memory.

After all, Sylvia had taught so many students over the years, published recipes in the local papers, ran a catering company and cooking school, appeared on television and of course on my radio show. And she had so many friends who adored her cooking.

It seemed a shame, we both agreed, to fail to make Sylvia's recipes and recollections available to her past students, family and friends in published form, especially when they were all compiled and almost ready to publish.

After a few more fits and starts looking for help to finish the process of self-publishing, I had the good fortune through a close friend to find Katie Erickson (KatieEricksonEditing.com), our intrepid editor and project manager. Katie's knowledge and professionalism are what have made it possible to finally get Sylvia's recipes, cooking tips and personal anecdotes into print and into your hands.

It gives me great pleasure to finally be able to share them in this cookbook that bears the name of the radio series that Sylvia presented for so long on Nash Holos Ukrainian Roots Radio. It was such an honour and privilege to know and work with her all those years, as it is now to have this tidy compilation of her delightful presentations of recipes, tips and stories to share with you.

I hope that you will treasure this cookbook, and that you will enjoy many happy meals making these wonderful recipes and serving them to your friends and family. And, perhaps, that you will pass it down the generations.

Paulette MacQuarrie

Foreword

I first met Paulette MacQuarrie decades ago, when I was a relatively new author and she was a relatively new radio producer. Our friendship blossomed with our mutual love of Ukrainian culture, history and memory. She interviewed me many times on Nash Holos about my books (at www.calla.com), and Paulette was one of the first members of my online group for writers of Ukrainian heritage called Storyfriends. I selected her beautiful short story, "Christmas Missed," for the anthology, *Kobzar's Children: A Century of Untold Ukrainian Stories*, published in 2006 and still in print.

Paulette had long spoken of Sylvia's extensive collection of recipes and how she wanted to make a cookbook with them. I was looking forward to reading it.

When Paulette handed me the galley pages for *Ukrainian Food Flair,* I wasn't prepared for the emotional impact these recipes and anecdotes would have on me. My father had the Ukrainian beaten out of him at the English school he attended on the Canadian prairies in the 1930s, and he didn't want his daughters to suffer that same trauma, so I wasn't immersed in the culture as a kid. I had to go out and find it and teach it to myself.

I also married into the culture. My Ukrainian mother-in-law had a vast repertoire of Ukrainian dishes, but they weren't all written down, and even those she did write down were hard to figure out. When she died, a lot of her signature dishes died with her. As I flipped through the pages of this cookbook, I wept. Those recipes are here.

Anyone who loves good homecooked food will find this collection to be a treasure trove. To those of you who have a bit of Ukrainian in you, delving into this cookbook will be like biting into a bit of nostalgia. The recipes are simple, clearly written, delicious and wholesome. This collection is a balm to the soul. Whether you're of Ukrainian heritage or you just love good food, this cookbook is about to be your new best friend.

Marsha Forchuk Skrypuch

Appetizers & Beverages

Canapés with Radish and Chives

This is an original recipe that was featured in *The Vancouver Sun* some years ago. It keeps well for several days so it can be made ahead.

- **1 cup (8-oz package) cream cheese**
- **2 tbsp butter**
- **½ cup radishes, chopped**
- **½ cup chives or green onion, chopped**
- **½ tsp salt**
- **1 clove garlic, minced**

1. Cream cheese with butter, add chopped radish, chives, garlic and salt, and mix well by hand or whiz in a food processor.

2. Store, covered, in refrigerator.

3. Delicious on dark rye bread triangles, or cocktail pumpernickel squares.

Makes 1½ cups.

Tip: If using chives, remember that their onion flavour strengthens with time.

Stuffed Eggs with Mushroom Caps

This recipe calls for you to fill your stuffed eggs as desired. You can vary a basic filling by adding chopped crisp bacon, chopped ham, cooked chopped chicken livers, sardines, pickles, olives, dill, or celery. Delicious as an appetizer, and ideal for a light lunch and with a salad and crusty bread.

- **1 small onion, finely chopped**
- **¼ cup olive oil**
- **1 tsp salt (or to taste)**
- **3 cups sliced mushrooms**
- **1 cup whipping cream**
- **½ cup browned, buttered**
- **6 large hard-cooked eggs, halved and stuffed**
- **12 jumbo white mushrooms**
- **Bread crumbs**

1. Sauté chopped onion in oil until soft. Add salt.

2. Add sliced mushrooms to onions and cook over medium heat until tender.

3. Add cream and cook another 5 minutes (or longer for a thicker sauce). Set sauce aside.

4. Pull stems out of jumbo mushrooms. Top each stuffed egg half with a large mushroom cap, open side down (to enclose egg).

5. Arrange in a shallow baking dish and pour enough mushroom sauce around the eggs to cover the bottom of the dish completely.

6. Sprinkle mushroom caps lightly with browned buttered breadcrumbs.

7. Bake in a 350°F oven until completely heated through, about 20 minutes.

Makes 12 appetizers.

Eggs with Caviar

Here is a very pretty Ukrainian appetizer that is always a hit at parties. Variations are endless, but I like it with caviar the best. The ultimate caviar is beluga—roe from the huge sturgeon. But it's extremely expensive, hundreds of dollars for a small tin! If that is beyond your budget, as it is for most people, you can substitute salmon roe, which is much less expensive. You can also use lumpfish roe. Although it's not a true caviar, it will work well in this recipe.

Variations: Top eggs with thinly sliced strips of smoked salmon, cooked shrimp or prawns, smoked oyster or cooked bay scallops. You can also mix hard boiled egg yolks with cooked chicken livers, minced ham, chicken or cheese. Use your imagination and experiment!

- **6 large hard cooked eggs cut in half lengthwise**
- **4 chives or green onions, very finely chopped**
- **2 tbsp mayonnaise, preferably Hellmann's**
- **1 tsp Dijon mustard**
- **3-4 tbsp caviar**
- **Salt to taste**
- **Dill sprigs, watercress and lettuce leaves for garnish**

1. Remove the yolks and mash until smooth.
2. Add onions or chives, mayonnaise and mustard.
3. Mix and season to taste with salt.
4. Stuff the egg white shells with yolk mixture.
5. Spoon a little caviar or other topping of choice on every egg.

Makes 12 appetizers.

Canapés with Bacon and Ham

This rich old-world recipe has long been prized for its flavour. Legend has it that it was a staple amongst traders (chumaky) in ancient times when several trading routes criss-crossed the steppes of what is now Ukraine. The chumaky needed food that kept well on long journeys through the wilderness. Smoked bacon, rye bread and garlic fit the bill very well.

At one time it was also accorded medicinal if not magical powers. It is said to form strong bonds of friendship between those who partake of it together.

- **2 tbsp salo* or side bacon, diced**
- **1 cup back bacon** or lean baked ham, diced**
- **3 cloves garlic, minced**
- **¼ tsp cayenne pepper (or to taste)**

1. Puree diced fat in a food processor, or mash using a mortar and pestle (as in the old days) until smooth.

2. Add bacon and garlic and process until shredded but not fine. Sprinkle with cayenne pepper.

3. Taste; the flavour should be smoky, smooth, and have a little "bite."

4. Chill, tightly covered, at least overnight. Keeps several days in the refrigerator.

5. Serve on rye or pumpernickel bread.

Makes just over one cup.

* Salo is non-rendered pork fat. You can find it in most East European delis. In a pinch, high-fat bacon with little meat can be used instead.
** Back bacon is known in some parts of the world as Canadian bacon.

Pickled Mushrooms

Pickled mushrooms go with just about any savoury dish and are very popular with Ukrainians. This quick and easy recipe is a great make ahead, and has a unique flavour that commercial products just can't duplicate.

- **1 lb small button mushrooms**
- **2 small onions, thinly sliced**
- **⅔ cup vinegar**
- **½ cup water**
- **1 whole bay leaf**
- **10 whole peppercorns**
- **1 tsp salt**
- **1 tsp sugar (or to taste)**
- **1 tbsp olive oil**

1. Clean and wash mushrooms, leaving stems on.

2. Cover with boiling salted water and cook for 15 minutes. Drain and cool.

3. Layer mushrooms and onion slices in a widemouth mason jar.

4. Simmer vinegar and water, bay leaf, peppercorns, salt and sugar.

5. Pour over mushrooms and onions.

6. Top with oil. Cover and let marinate in refrigerator for 1-3 days.

Makes about 4 cups.

Tip: Small fancy jars of little mushroom caps with pearl onions make a very elegant gift – especially for those who "have everything."

Stuffed Mushrooms

This recipe traditionally calls for Ukrainian bryndzia, a semi soft cheese made of ewe's milk favoured by the Hutsuls, who live in the Carpathian mountains. If you can't find bryndzia in a deli in your neighbourhood, Greek feta is a good substitute.

- **½ cup bryndzia or feta cheese, crumbled**

- **1 large hard-cooked egg, chopped**

- **1 clove garlic, mashed**

- **2 tbsp butter, soft**

- **12 large white mushrooms**

- **4 tbsp butter, melted**

1. Wipe mushrooms clean with a damp towel or cloth.

2. Mix cheese, egg, garlic and softened butter to blend.

3. Remove stems and reserve for later use.

4. Fill mushroom caps with cheese mixture. Brush with melted butter. Place on a baking sheet and broil 3-4 inches from heat until lightly browned, about 2 minutes.

Makes 1 dozen.

Navy Bean Dip

This flavourful dip is actually a traditional ritual Ukrainian Christmas dish, but is delicious at any time of year. Dried beans are best but if you're pinched for time, you can substitute canned beans. Serve this dip hot as a side dish, or cold as dip or a spread for canapés.

- **1 lb. dried white navy beans (2 cups)**
- **1 large onion, finely chopped**
- **¼ cup olive oil**
- **4 cloves garlic**
- **Salt & freshly ground pepper**

1. Soak beans overnight in water.
2. Drain softened beans, add fresh water to cover, and cook on low heat until tender, about 2½—3 hours.
3. Drain beans and mash.
4. Sauté onion in oil until very tender. Add to beans.
5. Mash garlic and add to bean mixture. Mix well.
6. Reheat and season to taste.

Makes about 3 cups.

Tip: When cooking beans, add a white onion to the pot for extra flavour.

Stuffed Cherry Tomatoes

Cottage cheese is widely used in Ukrainian cuisine in both sweet and savory dishes. This recipe will make your taste buds sing! It's a great make-ahead dish that adds a colourful festive touch to any table.

- **16 cherry tomatoes**
- **1 cup cottage cheese**
- **1 tsp finely chopped green onion or chives**
- **Salt to taste**
- **Parsley sprigs for garnish**

1. Wash tomatoes and slice off the tops.

2. With a teaspoon, scoop out the pulp and invert the tomatoes on paper towels to drain.

3. Mix the cheese, onion and salt in a bowl.

4. Stuff the tomatoes with the cheese mixture.

5. Arrange tomatoes on a platter on a bed of lettuce and garnish with parsley sprigs.

6. Refrigerate until ready to serve.

Makes 16 appetizers.

Cocktail Sausage Bites

It's always a great pleasure to have a piece of delicious Ukrainian garlic sausage (kovbasa in Ukrainian). Here's a quick recipe for your next party. It can't be any easier than this!

- **1 lb of lean ready-to-eat Ukrainian sausage**

- **¼ cup water**

1. Preheat your oven to 350°F.

2. Put the sausage in a shallow pan with the water.

3. Bake, uncovered, for 20 minutes or until the sausage has browned.

4. Remove from the oven, peel the casing and thinly slice. To serve, insert cocktail picks.

Serves a lot.

Tip: Ready-to-eat sausage can also be served without baking, but baking kovbasa brings out its fabulous flavour.

Asparagus Roll-ups

Asparagus has a delicate yet distinctive flavour, and its shape, whether svelte or plump, is always elegant. Make sure to use thin spears in this recipe because you are doubling them for each serving. This delicious appetizer is as delightful to eat as it is to look at.

- **8 slices roast beef, thinly sliced**

- **16 spears thin asparagus**

- **4 tbsp horseradish cream**

1. Wash and snap off tough ends of asparagus. Cook for 3 minutes in salted, boiling water until tender-crisp. Drain and pat dry with a paper towel.

2. Place two asparagus spear tips in opposite directions.

3. Spread each slice of roast beef lightly with prepared horseradish cream.

4. Wrap one slice roast beef around a pair of a asparagus and secure with a fancy toothpick.

Serves 8.

Tip: Ham, chicken, or smoked tongue can be used with equally delicious results.

Marinated Asparagus Spears

Asparagus grows so abundantly in Ukraine that it is considered a weed. Yet like many "weeds" it is nutritious and delicious, and so should be eaten often. This appetizer is particularly refreshing on a hot summer's day although it can of course be enjoyed any time of the year.

- **2 lbs cooked asparagus spears**
- **4 tbsp vinegar**
- **1½ tbsp salt**
- **4 cups water, boiled**
- **4 cloves garlic, sliced**
- **6 sprigs dill**
- **4 large eggs, hard-cooked, sliced**

1. Bring water, vinegar and salt to a boil. Cool.
2. Layer asparagus spears in a shallow dish with garlic and dill.
3. Cover asparagus with brine.
4. Marinate at room temperature overnight. Store in a covered container in refrigerator. (This will keep in the refrigerator for a couple of days.)
5. Serve drained asparagus over a bed of lettuce and garnish with hard-cooked egg slices.

Serves 6.

Tip: A good rule of thumb to follow when determining serving sizes for asparagus is to allow either 3 thick or 5 thin spears per person.

Ikra (Mock Caviar)

This traditional Ukrainian eggplant spread does not contain fish eggs, but it looks very much like real caviar! It's why ikra is often called "mock caviar," or "poor man's caviar." It's delicious served on crusty white or peasant rye bread. It makes an excellent side dish as well as an appetizer.

- **1 large globe or pear-shaped purple eggplant**
- **1 large onion, finely chopped**
- **4 tbsp olive oil**
- **2 tbsp tomato paste**
- **2 tbsp lemon juice, or to taste**
- **2 tsp salt**
- **Freshly ground black pepper**

1. Bake eggplant at 375°F, about 30-35 minutes or until soft when pierced with a knife. (Alternatively, cover eggplant with water and boil until tender, about 20 minutes.) Cool.

2. While the eggplant is cooking, fry onions in the oil until very soft.

3. When the eggplant has cooled, cut it in half. Scrape out the pulp, and mash with a fork. Do not remove the seeds.

4. Add the onions and sprinkle with lemon juice, salt and pepper. Add tomato paste and more oil if needed to make the spread lovely and smooth.

5. Store in a covered jar in the fridge. It will keep for several days, and flavour improves with age!

Makes about 3 cups.

Tip: A nice variation is to add 3-4 ripe, peeled and chopped tomatoes to the onion while it's cooking, and 2-3 smashed cloves of garlic to the eggplant mixture.

Pickled Herring (Ukrainian Style)

As a child, I remember eating raw salted herring with my dad – which didn't particularly impress my mom and sister. However, that was okay with me, because it meant more for my dad and me.

Meanwhile, Mom would pickle any salted herring that Dad and I didn't devour. To this day, I still pickle herring and make herring spread and salad. Although not common in modern day cookery in North America, it is actually quite easy, and well worth the effort.

- **6 herring fillets, in oil**
- **1 medium onion, sliced thin**
- **⅔ cup vinegar**
- **⅓ cup water**
- **⅓ cup sugar**
- **1 tbsp pickling spice**
- **1 whole bay leaf**
- **1 tbsp oil**

1. Combine water, vinegar and sugar in a pot and bring to a boil.
2. Cool and add pickling spice and bay leaf.
3. Slice herring fillets into 1-inch slices.
4. Layer alternately with onion slices in a sterilized jar. Add oil.
5. Pour vinegar mixture over top to cover, leaving a ½-inch space to the top.
6. Cover and marinate for 4 days in refrigerator.

Makes about 3 cups.

Tip: You can get herring fillets at most Mediterranean or European delis.

Herring in Mustard Sauce

Like all fish, herring is highly nutritious. It's a great source of vitamins A, D and B12, and essential fatty acids. It is also a traditional Ukrainian favourite and certainly one of mine. I have very fond memories of my recent trip to Ukraine, where I was able to indulge my passion for herring. This recipe is similar to a dish I enjoyed in Ukraine. It's easy to make and wickedly delicious.

- **16 oz. prepared pickled herring**

- **6 tbsp olive oil**

- **3 tbsp prepared mustard**

- **3 tbsp sour cream**

1. Cut herring into one-inch slices. Arrange in a shallow bowl.

2. Mix oil, mustard and sour cream to blend. Pour over the herring.

3. Chill for 2-3 hours before serving.

4. Serve on rye or pumpernickel bread, with a generous sprinkling of finely chopped hardcooked egg and chopped chives or green onion.

Serves 8.

Tip: Store-bought pickled herring works fine in this recipe, but if you want to be truly authentic, use your own home-made!

Prawns Kyiv

This recipe is a contemporary North American twist on a traditional recipe that ironically has no Ukrainian roots. No one knows for certain the actual origins of Chicken Kiev; however, being named after Ukraine's capital city, Ukrainians around the world adopted it as their own. This recipe for Prawns Kyiv reflects both the modern spelling of Ukraine's capital, and the Ukrainian propensity for adventurous adaptations!

- **3 oz butter, softened**
- **2 tsp seeded mustard**
- **1 tbsp flat-leaf parsley**
- **4 cloves garlic, mashed**
- **20 jumbo prawns**
- **Flour for dusting**
- **2 large eggs, slightly beaten**
- **⅓ cup milk**
- **Fine breadcrumbs for coating**
- **Oil for deep frying**

1. Mix butter with garlic, parsley and mustard.

2. Place mixture onto foil and shape into a 10 inch roll. Wrap in plastic wrap. Refrigerate until firm.

3. When firm, cut butter into 10 slices.

4. Shell and devein prawns. Place 2 prawns together between 2 sheets of plastic wrap. Pound gently into a flat circle. Repeat with remaining prawns.

5. Mold each prawn circle around each butter slice. (Using slightly wet hands will help.)

6. Toss the prawns in flour, shaking off any excess flour. Combine eggs and milk. Dip prawns into egg and milk mixture, then into breadcrumbs.

7. Place finished prawns on parchment paper and cool in the refrigerator for 30 minutes.

8. Shallow or deep fry in hot oil (375°F) until cooked through and golden, about 2 minutes per side.

Makes 10 appetizers.

Black Sea Sardine Spread

Sardines from the Black Sea have long been popular in Ukraine – fresh, salted, smoked, or canned in oil or tomato or mustard sauce. Try this traditional recipe for a surprisingly rich and flavourful canapé spread.

- **1 small can sardines in oil**
- **½ cup butter**
- **1 cup sour cream**
- **2 eggs hard-cooked, sieved**
- **2 green onions, finely chopped**
- **Juice of ½ lemon**
- **Salt & freshly ground pepper**

1. Mash the sardines to a smooth paste.

2. Add remaining ingredients, creaming until the mixture is smooth and well-blended. (A food processor makes this step very easy.)

3. Chill.

4. Spread on rye bread rounds or squares, and garnish with more chopped green onion or chives. Chopped red, yellow or white onion can also be used.

Makes about 2½ cups.

Tip: In Canada, sardines commonly come in cans of 106 grams. If you are using a different sized can, make sure to adjust the proportions of the other ingredients accordingly.

Smoked Fish Canapés

This is a modern adaptation of a traditional recipe. Any smoked or canned fish can be used, such as sprats, trout or, for a west-coast flavour, BBQ or smoked salmon. Serve on slices of your favourite cocktail deli bread.

- **8 oz. cream cheese**
- **6 oz. smoked fish**
- **2 eggs, hard-cooked**
- **Pinch paprika**

Garnishes:

- **Sardine fillets**
- **Dill pickles**
- **Radish**
- **Cucumber**
- **Peppers**
- **Cherry tomatoes**
- **Parsley, chives or fresh dill**

1. Cream cheese, smoked fish, and paprika into a smooth paste. Cover and refrigerate 2 hours.

2. Cut bread into desired fancy shapes.

3. Cut eggs, pickles and vegetables into various shapes – rounds, wedges and strips.

4. Place a dollop of the fish mixture on cut bread, top with a sardine fillet and/or any other desired garnishes.

Makes about 2 cups of filling.

Tip: Toasting the bread will give these appetizers a more intense flavour and crunchier texture.

Chicken Liver Spread

This is a family favourite that my sister and I grew up on. For a quick modern method, just put all the ingredients in the food processor, whiz a few times until smooth and creamy. Either way, you have a delicious and elegant spread.

- **1 lb chicken livers**
- **1 large egg, hard-cooked**
- **1 tbsp grated onion**
- **2 tbsp butter**
- **Salt & freshly ground pepper**

1. Simmer chicken livers in lightly salted water until done, about 6 minutes. Be careful not to overcook; they are done when they are just slightly pink. Drain.

2. Chop livers very fine. Add sieved egg and blend well.

3. Fry onion in butter until tender but not brown.

4. Put onion and the liver and egg mixture into a food processor and blend until smooth.

5. Season to taste. Add a little milk or cream if it's too thick to spread.

6. Serve on crackers or rye, pumpernickel, or crusty white bread.

Makes about 2 cups.

Tip: Chicken livers are the only livers that can be salted without getting hard, tough or grainy during cooking.

Mushroom Fritters

These fritters are lovely served with a dollop of tartar or horseradish sauce.

- **12 large mushrooms**
- **1 tsp salt**
- **2 eggs, beaten**
- **½ cup flour**
- **1-2 cups fine dry breadcrumbs**
- **Oil for frying**

1. Wipe mushrooms clean with a slightly damp cloth or paper towel.

2. Cut off the stems level with the mushroom.

3. Mix eggs and salt.

4. Dip the mushrooms first in the flour, next in egg and salt mixture, and then in breadcrumbs to coat.

5. Dry on racks for 20 minutes. (This will help keep oil from soaking into the coating.)

6. In a large skillet, shallow fry the mushrooms in hot (375°F) oil until golden.

7. Remove and drain on absorbent paper.

Makes 12 fritters.

Quick Garlic Puffs

This is the ultimate appetizer for garlic lovers. The recipe calls for frozen bread dough (white is best) but you can use your own home-made dough or purchase some from your favourite baker. In Ukrainian, these are called pampushky. Traditionally, pampushky are not fried, but baked as tiny dinner buns and drizzled with oil and crushed garlic. So for a lower-fat version, go traditional!

- **1 loaf frozen bread dough**
- **3 cloves garlic, mashed**
- **1 tbsp salt**
- **Olive or sunflower oil**

1. Thaw bread dough according to instructions.

2. Mash garlic cloves with salt. (The salt draws out the juice, and the flavour.)

3. Take a small piece of dough and roll between your lightly oiled palms into a 1-inch ball, and place on a floured towel.

4. Shallow fry balls in a skillet with 2 inches of hot (375°F) oil on all sides until golden. Do not overcrowd.

5. Remove with a slotted spoon, and drain on paper towels.

6. Drizzle with olive or sunflower oil (if desired).

7. Roll in mashed garlic or drizzle with garlic oil.

Makes about 2 dozen.

Tip: To make garlic oil, mash 2 heads of garlic with 1 tablespoon salt and mix with one cup oil. Please note that any oil or dressing containing fresh garlic can be kept in the fridge for up to 5 days (but if kept any longer, it could go rancid).

Pink Pickled Eggs

Pickled eggs are a delicious and nutritious snack. At one time they were as common in taverns as potato chips are today. Beets make these pickled eggs pink and pretty, and are sure to be a conversation piece at your next party.

- **1 dozen eggs, hard-cooked**
- **1 can sliced beets (14 oz.)**
- **1 cup vinegar**
- **1 cup water**
- **1 tbsp salt**
- **2 tbsp sugar**
- **1 small onion, sliced**
- **2 cloves garlic**
- **3 sprigs dill**

1. Remove shells from eggs and rinse.
2. Slice onion and place in a large sterilized jar with garlic, dill and beets (including juice).
3. Add eggs.
4. Boil vinegar, water, salt and sugar together. Cool.
5. Add cooled brine to the eggs and vegetables to cover.
6. Store in the refrigerator for 1 week before serving.

Makes 1 dozen pickled eggs.

Pyrizhky (Cocktail Buns)

These delicious Ukrainian pastries come stuffed with a sweet or savoury filling. The dough can be a yeast-raised bread or flaky dough, or a short or puff pastry. Busy contemporary cooks often use ready-to-use biscuit dough or puff pastry, and for yeast-raised pyrizhky, frozen bread dough or bread maker dough. The savoury fillings are often the same as for perogies and can be adjusted or combined to your individual taste. So be creative! But, be cautious when eating these pastries. Pyrizhky are highly addictive! They're fun to make, and a great make-ahead, as they can be frozen and reheated.

Basic method for yeast-raised pyrizhky

1. Roll out dough to about ¼ inch thickness.

2. Cut into 4-inch squares.

3. Place a rounded teaspoon or more of filling in the centre of the square.

4. Bring the two opposite edges together. Seal in a neat ridge, forming an oval.

5. Place on a greased baking sheet (sealed side down), 1-2 inches apart.

6. Cover and let rise in a warm place about 1 hour.

7. Brush with a beaten egg mixed with 2 tablespoons water or milk. Bake at 375°F for 30-35 minutes.

An elegant variation – Open-Faced Pyrizhky

1. Cut short or puff pastry (either homemade or store-bought) into 4-inch squares.

2. Put a rounded teaspoon or more of filling in centre of square.

3. Instead of creating an oval, bring the four corners of the square together in the centre and pinch them together.

4. Make sure the pinched join is at the centre top and the filling shows through in the four openings.

5. Place on a greased baking sheet (sealed side up).

6. Brush with a beaten egg mixed with 2 tablespoons water or milk. Bake at 400°F for 15-20 minutes.

Savoury Fillings for Pyrizhky

Sauerkraut:
Drain, rinse and squeeze out 1 large can of sauerkraut. Chop finely. Sauté 1 large finely chopped onion in ¼ cup butter or oil. Add sauerkraut and cook over medium heat about 30 minutes. Add salt and freshly ground pepper to taste. For ultimate flavour, add 1 tsp. sugar.

Cheese:
Mix together 1 lb farmer's cheese or dry cottage cheese, 1 egg, and salt and freshly ground pepper to taste. Cream cheese or sour cream may be added to taste.

Mushroom:
This filling is often used for vushka, the tiny dumplings served in clear borshch during the Christmas season. Sauté 1 finely chopped onion in 2 tbsp butter or oil until tender. Add 1 lb mushrooms, finely chopped. Sauté until tender, stirring occasionally. Season to taste with salt, freshly ground pepper and chopped dill. Stir in 1 slightly beaten egg yolk and mix well.

Cabbage:
Chop ½ head cabbage finely, boil in a little water in a tightly covered pan for 8 minutes. Drain thoroughly. Sauté 1 chopped onion in 2 tbsp butter or oil. Add cabbage, season to taste with salt and freshly ground pepper. Sauté until just warmed.

Meat:
Mix 1 lb cooked ground meat with a medium onion, finely chopped and sautéed in butter, oil or bacon fat. (If desired, sauté a bit of minced garlic with the onion.) Add a little gravy or soup stock to moisten. Season to taste with salt and pepper, and if desired, parsley or dill.

Potato and Dill:
To about 2 cups mashed potatoes, add 2 tbsp melted butter, 4 tbsp flour, one beaten egg yolk, ½ tsp grated onion or ¼ tsp onion powder, and 2 tbsp chopped fresh dill. Season with salt and pepper to taste.

Salo

In Europe, real lard made from rendered pork fat has always been a delicacy. In Ukraine, unrendered pork fat ("salo" in Ukrainian) is so highly favoured that it has earned the nickname "Ukrainian cocaine." Recently, as a novelty, they even began dipping it in chocolate!

Traditionally, Ukrainians slice salo fine and eat it on rye bread. They chop it with garlic and add it to borshch. They add it to sausage. They melt it down to fry sunflower seeds in, then use the cracklings to crumble over potatoes, perogies, cabbage rolls, or any number of savoury dishes. Try this simple yet delicious preparation for salo and take your taste buds on a real adventure!

- **1 slab pork belly fat, with skin, about 5 inches long**
- **1 large garlic clove**
- **2 tbsp sweet Hungarian paprika**

1. Pierce the slab with a sharp knife in 4-5 places.
2. Slice garlic clove and insert slices into the slits.
3. Cook in boiling water until fork-tender, about an hour.
4. Remove from water and pat dry.
5. Smear the slab generously with paprika. Roll and press the paprika into the slab.
6. Wrap and store in the refrigerator until ready to use. Keeps several weeks.
7. To serve, slice thinly (or shave) and serve on crackers or rye or pumpernickel bread.

Serves a lot.

Tip: Save the cooking liquid for a fabulous soup stock.

Cottage Cheese Dip

This delicious dip is low in calories but high in flavour. Serve with crackers, carrot or celery sticks, or spread on rye or pumpernickel bread and sprinkled with paprika.

- **2 cups creamed cottage cheese**
- **2 tbsp thick sour cream**
- **2 tsp chopped fresh dill**
- **1 tsp chopped green onion or chives**
- **¼ tsp caraway seed (optional)**
- **1 large egg, hard-cooked**
- **Salt to taste**

1. Press the cottage cheese through a sieve or whiz in a food processor.

2. Blend well with the cream and egg.

3. Mix in the other ingredients. Season to taste.

4. Chill.

Makes about 2½ cups.

Ultimate Party Paté

This delicate Ukrainian paté is always welcomed for the appetizer course. Lovely served with crusty white bread or baguette.

- **8 ounces of smoked bacon slices**
- **8 ounces of lean ground pork**
- **13 oz boneless chicken breast skinned**
- **1/2 a small onion, very finely chopped**
- **1 tbsp lemon juice**
- **2 eggs, beaten**
- **2 tbsp chopped flat leaf parsley**
- **1 tsp salt**
- **1 tsp peppercorns, crushed or 1/2 tsp freshly ground pepper**

1. Preheat oven to 325°F.

2. Arrange the bacon slices overlapping over the base and sides of a 2 pound loaf pan.

3. Cut about four ounces of the chicken breast into 4 inch strips. Set aside.

4. Put the remaining chicken, ground pork and onion in a food processor and process until smooth.

5. Add the eggs, parsley, salt and peppercorns to the meat mixture and pulse a few times.

6. Spoon half the mixture into the pan and arrange the chicken strips on top, then cover with the rest of the meat mixture.

7. Cover pan with a piece of well oiled foil. Place the foil covered pan in a larger roasting pan and place it in a 325°F oven. Pour enough hot water in the roaster pan to come half way up the sides of the loaf pan. This method (known as bain-marie) of placing the pan inside another larger pan filled to half with hot water ensures even cooking.

8. Bake at 325°F for 50 minutes or until firm.

9. Garnish with lettuce leaves, cherry tomatoes, radishes and lemon wedges.

Makes one loaf.

Fruity Buttermilk Shake

Because of its name and rich texture, many people think buttermilk is high in fat. But it's just the opposite. Originally, it was the liquid ("milk") leftover after cream was turned into butter. Today, buttermilk is commercially made by adding special (beneficial) bacteria to nonfat or low-fat milk, giving it a thicker texture and tangy flavour.

This drink is very much like a milkshake, but with a much lower fat content. I recommend using cherry, raspberry, apricot, peach or grape juice. You can also substitute yoghurt or a mixture of nonfat milk and yoghurt for the buttermilk. This will give you many varieties of this low-fat, high flavour treat.

- **2 cups buttermilk**
- **1 cup fruit juice**
- **2 tbsp sugar (or to taste)**

1. Combine all ingredients.

2. Stir well (or shake) until sugar is dissolved. (Use a blender if making large quantities.)

3. Chill thoroughly before serving.

Makes 3 cups.

Peperivka (Peppered Whiskey)

An interesting and long-standing tradition in Ukraine is spicing whiskey. Some say it's because spicing masked the poor quality of home-made brews (samohonka in Ukrainian). It may be more likely, however, that it's because the fierce bite peppers add to alcoholic drink makes it even more potent.

Growing up, I always knew this drink as peperivka. Traditionally, however, spiced whiskey would have been called pertsivka , derived from peretz, the Ukrainian word for pepper. Peperivka comes from the English word for pepper, reflecting the growing influence of English on the Ukrainian language spoken in Canada.

My uncle Steve used to always put black pepper into his vodka or gin. He lived to be 90, and my family has always believed it is entirely possible that drinking spiced spirits contributed to his longevity. If you're not keen on taking a pepper shaker to your gin and tonic, yet find the idea of a spiced whiskey intriguing, try this easy recipe.

- **8 large dry cayenne pepper pods**

- **2 cups whiskey, rye, bourbon or scotch**

1. Place peppers in a clean, dry one-quart crock.

2. Add whiskey, cork and let steep about one week.

Makes 2 cups spiced whiskey.

Watermelon-tini

I was first introduced to small round watermelons by my Baba (grandmother) when I met her in Ukraine for the first time back in 1968. Today, of course, they are common in North American supermarkets. You can eat this as a complete dish, or you can take out the chunks and enjoy the juice as a watermelon-tini, Chernivtsi style. But be careful – it's potent!

- **1 4-5 lb round watermelon**
- **1 12-oz bottle vodka**

1. Remove rind from watermelon.

2. Cut up the flesh into chunks and place them in a shallow dish.

3. Douse with vodka. Add sugar to taste, if desired, for more sweetness.

4. Chill until icy.

Serves 8.

Apple Punch

This fruity drink is very refreshing although the vodka makes it very potent. For a non-alcoholic version, replace the vodka with ginger ale or other non-cola soda.

- **1 large orange**
- **1 large lemon**
- **1 cup sugar**
- **1 cup vodka**
- **4 cups apple juice**

1. Slice orange and lemon with peel, place in a bowl, sprinkled with sugar and refrigerate overnight.

2. In the morning, add the vodka and let stand at room temperature for about 4-5 hours.

3. Stir in the apple juice, and chill until serving.

Serves 8.

Vodka Punch

There is a saying, "he who drinks lives long." Of course, we can't say for sure whether that's really the case. And so, it's always wise to remember that, as with all things, moderation is the key.

- ⅓ cup water

- 3 whole peppercorns

- Zest of 1 lemon

- 2 tbsp buckwheat honey (or other dark honey)

- 2 tbsp sugar

- ½ cup water

- 2 cups vodka

1. Boil water, peppercorns and lemon zest in a medium saucepan. Lower heat and simmer for about 10 minutes.

2. Boil the honey, sugar and ½ cup water in a small pot. Remove any foam.

3. Mix the reserved liquid and honey mixture and add the vodka.

4. Heat on low. Pour into punch cups while warm.

Serves 6.

Cherry Vodka

Cherry vodka is my very favorite vodka drink. Once you taste this delicious drink, I'm sure it will be a favourite of yours as well.

- **2½ cups vodka**
- **4 tbsp orange zest**
- **10 whole cloves**
- **1¼ cups cherry syrup**

1. Put vodka, orange zest and cloves into a glass or non-reactive bowl.

2. Cover and keep at room temperature for 2 weeks.

3. Strain off vodka. Add the cherry syrup, mixing to blend well.

4. Store in sealed jars. This drink will keep for up to six months.

Makes about 4 cups.

Tip: Cherry and other fruit syrups (often home-made) were commonly used as a base for drinks in the days before commercially bottled soft drinks became widely available. Today you can find fruit syrups in most specialty food stores.

Tipsy Cranberries

Ukrainian cranberries, or kalyna, are also known as high-bush cranberry, which are smaller and more tart than the commercially grown bog cranberries familiar to North Americans. Happily, this recipe lends itself well to either variety. This sauce is great on cakes, puddings and ice cream.

- **4 cups fresh cranberries**
- **2 cups sugar**
- **⅓ cup brandy or rum**

1. Mix cranberries with sugar and bake in a shallow ovenproof dish at 325°F for 45 minutes.

2. Remove from oven and stir in brandy or rum.

3. Store, covered, in the refrigerator.

Makes 3 cups.

Soups & Accompaniments

Asparagus Soup

This unusual and delicious soup is easy to make and very elegant.

- **1 lb asparagus**
- **4 cups water or chicken stock**
- **1 tsp sugar**
- **2 tsp salt**
- **3 tbsp butter**
- **3 tbsp flour**
- **2 tbsp flat leaf parsley, finely chopped**
- **½ cup whole milk or cream (half & half)**
- **½ tsp salt, or to taste**

1. Clean asparagus and snap off tough ends. Cut asparagus into 1-inch pieces.

2. Add the sugar and salt to enough water to cover the asparagus. Drop in the asparagus pieces and simmer for 5 minutes, or until tender crisp. Drain.

3. Melt the butter in a heavy skillet, mix in the flour and parsley. Cook, stirring for about 3 minutes and dilute with milk or cream.

4. Gradually add water (or stock) and the asparagus pieces.

5. Adjust seasoning and simmer for about five more minutes, or until asparagus is done.

6. For a creamier soup, purée in a food processor.

7. Garnish with a dollop of sour cream.

Serves 5-6.

Tip: Instead of tossing the water, reserve it to add to the soup stock.

Spring Borshch

Spring borshch is made of tender young beets, which don't give as deep and dark a red colour to the borshch as mature beets. Hence the Ukrainian name for this borshch – "biliy" (meaning "white") borshch. This soup makes an excellent first course. Or, served with new potatoes, a traditionally favourite combination, it makes a satisfying light meal. Also delicious served with pyrizhky – baked pastries filled with meat, liver, cabbage or mushrooms.

- **3 large new beets with tops**
- **2 large celery ribs**
- **2 medium onions, chopped**
- **2 large carrots, diced**
- **2 small parsnips, diced**
- **1 cup shredded cabbage**
- **5 large fresh mushrooms**
- **1 tbsp oil**
- **2 tbsp flour**
- **4 cups chicken broth**
- **1 cup buttermilk**
- **1 cup sour cream**
- **1 tsp chopped fresh dill**
- **2 cloves garlic (or to taste)**
- **1 tsp salt**

1. Wash beets and tops well. Peel and shred the beetroot. Chop the tops and discard stems.

2. Add to broth along with chopped onion, carrots, parsnips and cabbage. Cook until soft.

3. Slice mushrooms and cook in oil. Stir in flour to make a paste. Add a little broth, bring to a light boil, then add to vegetables.

4. Mix in buttermilk and sour cream, and add to soup. Do not boil, as it may make the borshch curdle.

5. Taste and adjust seasoning.

6. Garnish with sprigs of fresh dill and, if desired, a pinch of garlic mashed with salt.

Serves 8-10.

Tip: To prevent curdling, add some dill to the broth before adding cream.

Vegetarian Borshch

Meatless borshch is traditionally served for Christmas Eve dinner (called Sviat Vechir), with wonderful little dumplings called vushka. However, it is delicious any time of year. When serving with vushka at Christmas Eve, strain or remove most of the vegetables.

- **1 large onion, finely chopped**
- **4 tbsp vegetable oil**
- **2 large carrots, shredded**
- **1 small parsnip, diced**
- **3 medium beets, julienne**
- **1 small cabbage, shredded**
- **1 large potato, diced**
- **1 small clove garlic, crushed (optional)**
- **6 cups water**
- **1 cup tomato juice**
- **1 small bay leaf**
- **Salt & freshly ground pepper**
- **Chopped fresh dill**

1. Sauté the onion in oil until slightly wilted.

2. Add the carrots, parsnips and beets and continue to sauté for 5 minutes.

3. Place in a soup pot along with remaining vegetables, garlic, water, tomato juice and bay leaf.

4. Cover and simmer until vegetables are soft, about one hour.

5. Remove bay leaf before serving.

Serves 10.

Tip: Borshch should never be boiled, but rather simmered slowly. Very freezer friendly!

Green Borshch

There are many recipes for borshch, Ukraine's national soup. They depend on the vegetables in season and local preferences.

One very different borshch is made with young, tender sorrel leaves. Sorrel is a unique, tangy herb that belongs to the buckwheat family. It can be cooked like spinach, or mixed with spinach or chard to add a sharp, lemony flavor. Sorrel grows wild in Ukraine but in North America it is cultivated in gardens.

Mr. Station, a chef at the Hotel Vancouver back in the 1940s and 1950s, introduced sorrel soup to the hotel's menu. He and his wife were friends of my parents and he gave Mom a sorrel plant from his garden. The sorrel plant in my own garden came from this plant.

This delectable borshch is a particular treat in the springtime, when sorrel is at its best.

- **3 cups young, tender sorrel leaves**
- **3 tbsp butter**
- **1 tsp salt (or to taste)**
- **3 tbsp flour**
- **7 cups chicken stock**
- **¾ cup cream**
- **¾ cup sour cream**
- **1½ cups cooked rice**
- **3 large hard-cooked eggs, sliced**

1. Trim stems from leaves, wash, drain and chop.
2. Sauté flour in melted butter until golden.
3. Add salt and sorrel, cook, stirring until wilted.
4. Add stock and cook until thickened.
5. Mix creams and slowly add to stock. Simmer 2 minutes.
6. Serve with a spoonful of cooked rice in each bowl. Garnish with egg slices.

Serves 8-10.

Tip: Half and half cream is fine but whipping cream gives a richer flavour.

Green Borshch — Sorrel & Vegetable

This hearty green borshch recipe is laden with vegetables and is delightfully tangy.

Sorrel leaves are very high in vitamin C and are delicious in soups and salads. As sorrel matures, it becomes more acidic, so it's best to use young leaves. Cooked sorrel can be used in soups, stews and sauces. It can be eaten raw in salads, but because of its tartness, it is usually mixed with other greens such as spinach.

If you don't have sorrel you could use a touch of vinegar or rhubarb juice as an acceptable substitute.

- **1 medium onion, finely chopped**
- **2 tbsp butter**
- **7 cups soup stock (chicken or vegetable)**
- **1 large potato, diced**
- **1 cup celery, chopped**
- **1 cup carrot, chopped**
- **1 cup cabbage, chopped**
- **3-4 cups sorrel, chopped**
- **2 tbsp flour**
- **¾ cup sour cream**
- **3 tbsp chopped fresh dill, or to taste**
- **Salt and pepper to taste**
- **4 hard-boiled eggs, halved**

1. Fry onion in butter until tender.
2. Add stock, potatoes, carrots, celery and cabbage. Cook until tender.
3. Strain vegetables and push through a sieve, or whiz in a food processor until smooth. Return to the stock pot.
4. Add sorrel and cook another 1-2 min.
5. Blend flour with sour cream into a smooth paste, stir into soup mixture and bring to a soft boil.
6. Add chopped dill and season to taste.
7. Place half an egg in each bowl and fill with borshch.

Serves 8.

Old-Time Potato Soup with Gravy

I always like to have a jar of browned flour on hand as it gives a special flavor to soups, stews and gravies. Luckily, I learned from Mom how to do it. It's really easy.

Just spread white flour about ¼" thick in the bottom of the heavy frying pan, place over medium heat, and stir often until the flour takes on an even tan color. Don't rush it and don't leave the frying pan because if you do it will burn in a minute!

Browned flour is what gives this potato soup its old-time Ukrainian flavour.

- **3 large potatoes, diced**
- **6 cups cold water**
- **½ pound bacon, diced**
- **1 large onion, sliced**
- **4 tbsp browned flour**
- **Salt and freshly ground pepper**

1. Boil potatoes in salted water until tender. Do not drain.

2. Fry bacon and onions until bacon is crisp and onions are soft.

3. Add browned flour to the bacon and onions, cook for five minutes.

4. Add to the potatoes and season to taste with salt and pepper.

Serves 6-7.

Cream of Cabbage Soup

Cabbage has sometimes been referred to as "poor man's vitamin C," but this highly nutritious vegetable has been prized in royal courts down the centuries. This delicious Ukrainian soup is easy to make and will impress friends and family, whatever their station in life.

- **1 medium head cabbage (about 3 lbs), shredded**
- **½ cup celery, diced**
- **½ cup onion, chopped**
- **4 cups chicken broth**
- **1 tsp salt**
- **½ tsp freshly ground pepper**
- **⅓ cup butter**
- **⅓ cup flour**
- **4 cups milk**

1. Combine first 6 ingredients in a soup pot and cover.

2. Heat to boiling over medium heat, and simmer for 20 minutes. Remove from heat.

3. In a saucepan, melt the butter and blend in the flour.

4. Gradually stir in the milk, cooking over medium heat, stirring until the mixture thickens and boils.

5. Add the milk mixture to the soup pot with the cabbage mixture, and cook over low heat for 5 minutes or till heated through.

Serves 10-12.

Chicken Soup with Tiny Dumplings

For ultimate flavour, make your own stock for this yummy soup (you can freeze any left over for later use). If you're in a hurry, however, organic store-bought soup stock is a reasonable substitute. But you won't likely find the delicious tiny dumplings (called halushky) that traditionally accompany this soup in any store. Fortunately, they're quick and easy to make!

- **6 cups chicken stock**
- **2 tbsp oil or butter**
- **1 large carrot, diced**
- **1 small parsnip, diced**
- **1 medium onion, finely chopped**
- **Fresh dill for garnish**
- **Salt to taste**

Dumplings:
- **1 large egg**
- **1 tbsp cold water**
- **½ cup flour**
- **Pinch of salt**

1. Heat chicken stock in a large pot.

2. Sauté vegetables in the oil or butter until tender-crisp. Add to the stock. Salt to taste.

3. To make the dumplings, beat egg with water and salt in a cup or small bowl.

4. Add flour and mix to form a soft dough.

5. Scoop up a little dough (about the size of a kidney bean) onto a small teaspoon and dip into gently (not rapidly!) boiling soup. Dumplings will slide off the spoon.

6. Dumplings are done when they float to the top.

7. Garnish soup with chopped dill and serve hot.

Serves 6-7.

Tip: These dumplings can be used in place of noodles or other pasta and served with a variety of soups, sauces, or gravies.

Hearty Sauerkraut Soup

Tangy and filling, this hearty sauerkraut soup (kapusnyak in Ukrainian) is delicious with fresh rye bread and butter. Add a bit of cream for a more mellow, and richer, flavour.

- **3 lbs fresh pork neck bones, ribs or oxtail**

- **8 cups water**

- **1 large onion, chopped**

- **3 whole bay leaves**

- **2 tsp whole black peppercorns**

- **3 cups sauerkraut, drained**

- **2 large potatoes, diced**

- **1 tsp salt (or to taste)**

1. Wash meat, place in a soup pot and cover with water.

2. Add peppercorns, onion, bay leaves.

3. Cover and simmer until meat is tender.

4. Add sauerkraut and potatoes.

5. Continue cooking until vegetables are tender. Remove bay leaves.

6. Taste, adjust for salt.

Serves 8-10.

Sauerkraut Soup with Buckwheat

This delicious, nutritious, low-calorie soup provides plenty of fibre as well as flavour. To make it extra special, use home-made sauerkraut, or a fermented variety imported from Eastern Europe. This soup freezes well, so you can double the recipe for a quick meal to have on hand.

- **3 tbsp oil**
- **1 large onion, finely chopped**
- **4 cups lean meat stock**
- **2 cups sauerkraut**
- **1 tsp black peppercorns**
- **2 cups cooked buckwheat**

1. Place meat stock, sauerkraut and peppercorns in a soup pot. Bring to a boil.
2. Fry onion in oil until soft. Add to soup pot.
3. Simmer 30 minutes.
4. Add cooked buckwheat.
5. Simmer another 5 minutes.
6. Season to taste and serve.

Serves 6.

Beef & Barley Soup

Pearl barley has had the bran removed and has also been steamed and polished. It comes in coarse, medium and fine, and is ideal for soups and stews. It blends beautifully with beef and vegetables in this hearty and flavourful soup (krupnyk), which takes its name from the Ukrainian word for "peeled grains."

- **2 lbs beef short ribs, cut into small pieces**
- **3 tbsp oil**
- **7 cups water**
- **⅔ cup pearl barley**
- **1 can diced tomatoes (14 oz)**
- **1 large onion, chopped**
- **2 tsp salt**
- **1 cup celery, sliced**
- **½ cup green pepper, chopped**
- **¼ cup parsley, finely chopped**

1. In a heavy skillet, brown short ribs in oil over medium high heat. (Or, roast in a hot oven until brown.)
2. Drain well.
3. Place ribs in a stock pot with water and barley.
4. Cover and cook about 1 hour.
5. Add remaining ingredients and simmer 45 minutes.
6. Skim off any fat, and season to taste.

Serves 8.

Fresh Mushroom Soup

Ukrainians are known for their love of mushrooms, especially wild ones. Some Ukrainians know exactly where, when and how to pick the right ones in the wild. This knowledge is coveted (and highly guarded!) by mushroom connoisseurs. It is very valuable, and goes beyond just knowing the "secret spots" for the best mushrooms – some fatally toxic wild mushrooms closely resemble the edible varieties and can fool any but the most experienced and knowledgeable mushroom pickers.

Fortunately for the rest of us, many varieties of wild mushrooms can now be found alongside cultivated mushrooms in most supermarkets and green grocers. This soup is delicious using either wild or cultivated varieties, or a combination.

- **1½ lbs fresh mushrooms, sliced**
- **1 large onion, finely chopped**
- **3 tbsp butter**
- **3 tbsp flour**
- **2 large potatoes, diced**
- **1 small parsnip, sliced**
- **1 medium turnip, diced**
- **8 cups water or chicken stock**
- **Salt and freshly ground pepper**

1. Sauté the mushrooms and onions in butter, cooking until onions become soft.
2. Sprinkle with flour and mix.
3. Cook the other vegetables in water or stock until done.
4. Add the mushroom-onion mixture, stirring while bringing to a boil.
5. Season to taste and continue to cook over medium heat for 10 minutes.
6. Pureé soup if desired.

Serves 8-10.

Mushroom Barley Soup

Mushrooms add an intense flavour to this soup rich with barley and vegetables.

- **1 lb mushrooms, sliced**
- **6 tbsp butter**
- **½ cup pearl barley**
- **1 large onion, chopped**
- **2 cloves garlic, chopped**
- **2 large carrots, sliced**
- **1 large potato, diced**
- **2 whole bay leaves**
- **6 cups beef stock**
- **¼ cup dill, chopped**
- **½ cup sour cream**
- **Salt and freshly ground pepper**

1. Sauté onions in butter until soft.
2. Add the garlic and continue to cook one minute.
3. Add remaining ingredients, bring to a boil, then reduce heat and simmer for 1 hour.
4. Taste and adjust seasonings. Remove bay leaves before serving.
5. Serve with a dollop of sour cream.

Serves 6-8.

Home-made Noodles for Milk Soup

Milk soup is made by cooking a small quantity of cereals in milk, such as rice, buckwheat groats, millet, pearl barley, coarse farina, or cornmeal. We also enjoyed home-made egg noodles (lokshyna) in our milk soup. These soups can be seasoned with salt or a small amount of sugar. Dad always salted his milk soup, but my sister and I preferred the sugar, as we loved the sweet skin that formed on the top of the soup. Here's my family's recipe for milk soup with home-made egg noodles. These noodles are also wonderful with chicken soup, and any dish calling for noodles.

- **2 large eggs, beaten**
- **1 tbsp water**
- **1½ cups flour**
- **1 tsp salt**
- **2 cups milk (or more)**
- **Salt or sugar to taste**

1. Mix eggs, water, flour and salt and form into a smooth, stiff dough. Cover and let sit for 10 minutes.

2. Roll out dough as thin as possible without breaking, on a floured surface.

3. Let the dough dry for 5 minutes, then dust top of dough lightly with flour.

4. For long noodles, roll dough up as for a jelly roll, and slice into thin strips with a very sharp knife. For short noodles, cut the dough into 2-inch strips. Stack strips on top of each other and slice into thin strips.

5. Boil noodles for 10 minutes in salted water.

6. Meanwhile, put milk in a saucepan or double boiler and bring to a gentle boil.

7. When noodles are cooked, strain and toss to separate. Add desired amount to hot milk. Season soup with salt or sugar and serve.

Serves 2-3.

Milk Soup with Egg Drops

Egg drops cooked in milk are true Ukrainian comfort food! This is a variation of the milk soup with egg noodles. Egg drops are actually simple little dumplings made by pouring batter from a spoon into simmering milk, or any kind of soup.

This recipe is not precise, as the amount of the ingredients will depend on how much soup and how many dumplings you want to serve.

Oddly enough, these little dumplings are also called barley drops, even though they contain no barley. How they got this name is still an unsolved mystery!

However there is no mystery to making them. They are easy and fun to make, and even more to eat!

- **1-2 cups milk**
- **1 egg**
- **1 tbsp water**
- **4 tbsp flour**
- **Pinch of salt**

1. Bring milk to a gentle simmer in a pot.

2. In a separate bowl, beat the egg and then beat in the remaining ingredients to form a smooth, thick batter.

3. Pour slowly from the end of a spoon in a thin stream over simmering soup or milk and allow to cook for two to three minutes. If poured from a height, you'll get a better shape to the egg drops.

4. Serve hot.

Serves 2-3.

Jellied Beet Borshch

Jellied beet borshch is wonderful for a late lunch on a hot summer day. It also makes a beautiful appetizer.

The best part is that it only takes about 15 minutes to make.

- **4 cups borshch (purchased or homemade), with shredded beets**

- **¼ cup fresh lemon juice**

- **¼ tsp salt**

- **5 tsp unflavored gelatin**

1. Sieve the borshch into a large saucepan and keep the beets for another use.

2. Stir in lemon juice, salt, and sprinkle with gelatin. Let stand for a minute to soften the gelatin.

3. Bring to a boil, stirring, and pour into a 9 inch glass container.

4. Cover and chill until set, about 4—4½ hours.

5. Dice and serve in bowls with very finely diced radish and cucumber, some chopped fresh dill and a dollop of sour cream.

Serves 4-6.

Chilled Borshch Smetana

Chilled soups are always great in the summer! Ukrainians love borshch, either hot or cold. There certainly are many delicious recipes for both types.

Cold borshch is very easy to make and very popular in Ukraine to this day, as I discovered when I visited there recently.

This delicious and refreshing soup with beets and sour cream (smetana) is very elegant, yet a snap to prepare.

- **3 beets cooked**

- **1 slicing cucumber, peeled**

- **1 cup cream (10%)**

- **3 large hard-cooked eggs, chopped**

- **1 tbsp green onion, finely chopped**

- **2 tbsp fresh dill, finely chopped**

- **2 cups sour cream**

- **Salt & freshly ground pepper**

1. Grate the beets and cucumber coarsely.

2. Add the cream, eggs, green onion, and dill. Mix.

3. Add 1½ cups of the sour cream, and season to taste.

4. Chill thoroughly.

5. Serve cold in chilled soup bowls with an extra dollop of sour cream.

Serves 4-5.

Chilled Vegetable Soup

Buttermilk and sour cream enhance the flavour of the vegetables in this chilled savoury soup, making it satisfying as well as refreshing.

- **4 cups buttermilk**
- **½ cup sour cream**
- **1 cup cooked diced beets**
- **1 cup peeled and diced cucumber**
- **1 cup diced boiled potatoes**
- **2 tbsp grated raw carrot**
- **2 tbsp chopped green onion**
- **2 tbsp chopped fresh dill**
- **3 large hard-cooked eggs, chopped**
- **Salt & freshly ground pepper**

1. Beat the buttermilk and sour cream together until smooth.

2. Add remaining ingredients and season to taste with salt and pepper.

3. Chill thoroughly before serving. (Chill your soup bowls, too!)

Serves 6-8.

Chilled Cucumber Soup

This delicious Ukrainian cucumber soup has been around a long time. It's quick and easy, but if you want it even quicker and easier, just whiz all the ingredients in a food processor. Then pour, garnish, and serve.

- **2 large seedless cucumbers, peeled**
- **4 green onions, chopped**
- **8 red radishes, finely chopped**
- **4 tbsp lemon juice**
- **1 tsp salt (or to taste)**
- **1 tbsp chopped fresh dill**
- **4 cups water, approximately**
- **Sour cream or yoghurt, to garnish**

1. Grate cucumbers.
2. Mix with chopped onion, radish, lemon juice, salt and water to cover.
3. Taste to adjust seasoning.
4. Sprinkle with dill and chill thoroughly.
5. Garnish with a dollop of sour cream or yoghurt.

Serves 6.

Tip: I recommend using long English cucumbers, which are readily available in North American supermarkets, for this soup.

Chilled Summer Sorrel Soup

This soup is made with the young tender leaves of sorrel, a perennial plant that appears in early spring. It grows in clumps similar to spinach, and is known for its sour taste. It grows wild in Ukraine, but fortunately it is very easy to grow in your garden.

This easy to prepare and deliciously refreshing soup has long been a traditional Ukrainian favourite.

- **25 young sorrel leaves, washed and stems removed**

- **1 medium onion, finely chopped**

- **8 cups water, chicken or beef stock**

- **4 large hard-cooked eggs, separated**

- **½ cup cream**

- **2 medium cucumbers – peeled and thinly sliced**

- **1 tbsp chopped fresh dill**

1. Bring sorrel, onion, water or stock to the boil in a soup pot and simmer 10 min. Cool.

2. Blend the yolks with cream. Set aside. Chop egg whites finely.

3. To serve, pour soup into a deep bowl.

4. Add chopped egg whites, cucumber slices and chopped dill.

5. Garnish with a dollop of egg yolk mixture.

Serves 6.

Chilled Fruit Soup

Serving cold soup on a hot day is a cherished old-country tradition in Ukraine. It is so refreshing and nourishing, and an imaginative cook can create an endless number of delicious variations. These soups can also be served as a dessert if you make them just a little bit sweeter.

- **3 cups fresh fruit – cherries, plums, peaches, apricots, apples, or a combination**
- **6 cups boiling water**
- **1 cup whipping cream**
- **½ cup sugar (or to taste)**
- **Lemon juice to taste**
- **Grated lemon zest**

1. Place fruit and boiling water in a large pot and cook until fruit is soft.

2. Remove fruit and press through a sieve. Pour any leftover liquid back into the pot along with the pureéd fruit.

3. Bring soup back to a boil. Sweeten to taste, and add some lemon juice for a sweettartness.

4. Cool and stir in enough cream to get the desired creamy consistency.

5. Chill thoroughly. Serve in well-chilled cups or soup bowls.

6. Garnish with some grated lemon rind as a first course or, for dessert, top with hrinky (sweet croutons).

Serves 6-8.

Assorted Dried Fruit Soup

Cold soups made from fresh and dried fruits are served as a first course in parts of Ukraine and as a dessert farther north. Some are like a very liquid compote with the fruit left whole or cut into pieces. Others are pureed. Either way, they are very refreshing soups! Here is a delicious soup using dried fruit. Choose any combination of your favorite fruits – prunes, dried apples, peaches, pears, raisins, cranberries – the sky's the limit!

- **¾ pound assorted dried fruit**
- **Half a stick cinnamon**
- **6 cups cold water**
- **¼ to ½ cup sugar or to taste**
- **Juice of ½ a lemon**
- **Grated lemon rind**

1. Wash the fruit in warm water. Drain. Place fruit in a large pot, add the cinnamon stick and the 6 cups of cold water.

2. Cook over low heat until the fruit is tender.

3. Remove the fruit and press it through a sieve. Set aside.

4. Meanwhile, add sugar to the juice and bring to a boil.

5. Stir in the lemon juice. Remove from heat and mix in the pureed fruit.

6. When cool enough, pour into a serving bowl. Chill thoroughly.

7. Sprinkle with grated lemon rind to serve.

Serves 6.

Strawberry Soup

Strawberries are always special to me because they are the first sign of summer. The taste of fresh strawberries is unbeatable, and lucky for us there are hundreds of ways to enjoy this fruit.

This chilled strawberry soup is very refreshing on a hot summer day, or any time of year. If you can't get fresh strawberries, frozen berries will work fine in this recipe.

- **5 cups fresh strawberries**
- **2 cups water**
- **⅔ cup sugar**
- **2 tbsp quick cooking tapioca**
- **1 cup yogurt plain or strawberry flavored**

1. Clean and hull strawberries. Save a few for garnish.

2. Puree in a blender or food processor until smooth. Place the puree in a large saucepan with water, sugar and tapioca.

3. Cook over medium heat until the mixture thickens, about 5 to 6 minutes.

4. Cool slightly and whisk in yoghurt. Refrigerate until thoroughly chilled.

5. Place a whole strawberry in each bowl to garnish.

Serves 6.

Chilled Apple Soup

This is a good basic recipe for sweet fruit soup. It calls for apples but any fruit can be used. Make a big batch, then freeze it in cartons so you will always have a very cold, refreshing soup at hand.

- **3 cups water**
- **4 large apples, peeled and diced**
- **½ cup sugar (or more to taste)**
- **1 tbsp lemon zest**
- **2-3 tbsp lemon juice**
- **2 tbsp cold water**
- **2 tbsp flour**
- **1 cup white wine**
- **½ cup heavy cream (optional)**

1. Combine water, apples, sugar, zest and lemon juice. (Omit lemon juice if fruit is already tart.) Cook until apples are tender.

2. Mix water and flour and add to soup. Simmer 5-6 minutes. Put soup through a strainer if it is seedy.

3. Stir in wine and adjust for desired sweetness.

4. Chill thoroughly. Add cream before serving, if desired.

5. Serve in chilled bowls.

Serves 4.

Sweet Croutons

These unusual croutons, called hrinky in Ukrainian, are simple to make, and pure fun! When I discovered this old country recipe I promptly fell in love with it. Serve with chilled fruit soups to give them an extra special touch – and impress your guests.

- **4 slices day-old bread**

- **1 large egg, beaten**

- **2 tbsp cream**

- **2 tbsp sugar**

1. Cut crusts off slices of day-old bread.

2. Cut each slice into 4 finger lengths.

3. Dip fingers in a mixture of slightly beaten egg and cream, then pan fry hot butter on both sides.

4. Sprinkle with sugar.

Makes 16 fingers.

Tip: A nice variation is to substitute sifted icing sugar for the granulated sugar.

Salads

Asparagus & Beet Salad

This salad is not only delicious, with its contrasting colours it is also a feast for the eyes. Beautiful and elegant on a buffet table or at formal sit-down dinners, and it is a great make-ahead.

- **1 lb asparagus**
- **¼ cup vinegar**
- **¾ cup vegetable oil**
- **¼ tsp dry mustard**
- **½ tsp salt**
- **3 tbsp green onion, diced**
- **1 cup beets, cooked and diced**
- **2 tbsp bryndzia, feta, or blue cheese, crumbled**
- **8 large eggs, hard-cooked**
- **Salad greens and red onion rings for garnish**

1. Wash asparagus and snap off tough ends. Cut asparagus into 1-inch pieces.

2. Cook asparagus until tender-crisp, in boiling salted water (about 5 minutes). Drain and chill.

3. Prepare the dressing by blending the vinegar, oil, mustard and salt. Mix in the green onion, cheese, beets and one diced egg.

4. Arrange asparagus on a platter surrounded by lettuce leaves.

5. Slice remaining eggs and place along with onion rings on the lettuce leaves.

6. Sprinkle with dressing.

Serves 6.

Cucumber & Dill Pickle Salad

This unusual combination is surprisingly delicious. Plus, it is super quick and easy to make. The fresh cucumbers, like all uncooked vegetables, contain beneficial enzymes which are lost through heat processes such as pasteurization and pickling. For more enzymes, use unpasteurized honey and the fermented variety of pickles.

- **2 cups seedless cucumber, peeled and diced**
- **2 cups dill pickles, diced**
- **⅓ cup honey, or enough to coat**

1. Toss diced vegetables with honey.

Serves 5-6.

Beet & Dill Pickle Salad

Simple, and easy to make, this tangy salad is an elegant addition to any table. The horseradish gives it a nice bite, and sunflower oil enhances the earthy taste of the beets.

- **8 large beets, cooked and sliced**
- **3 large dill pickles, sliced**
- **1 large onion, sliced**
- **3 tbsp prepared horseradish**
- **4 tbsp sunflower (or olive) oil**

1. Mix horseradish and oil.
2. Pour over vegetables.
3. Toss and serve.

Serves 8-10.

Bukovynian Supper Salad

Bukovyna is the region in Ukraine where my mom is from. I visited there twice. The first time was in 1968 to find my Baba (grandmother). The second time, just a few years ago, I went again to revisit beautiful Bukovyna and find my cousin.

I discovered this wonderful recipe on that second trip. This Bukovynian-style salad is hearty enough to be a meal in itself.

- **1 lb Ukrainian sausage, cooked and sliced**
- **4 large potatoes, cooked and diced**
- **2 large carrots, cooked and diced**
- **2 large green peppers, thinly sliced**
- **1 bunch green onions, sliced**
- **1 cup cut green beans, cooked**
- **1 cup mayonnaise**
- **Salt & freshly ground pepper**

1. Mix all ingredients.
2. Season to taste.

Serves 8.

Tip: If you can't find Ukrainian sausage, substitute any other European-style smoked sausage.

Cucumber Salad

The small amount of sugar contrasts with the vinegar and gives this traditional cucumber salad (called mizeria in Ukrainian) a nice, tangy twist.

- **3 large cucumbers**
- **1 tsp salt**
- **1 medium onion, sliced thin**
- **½ cup sour cream**
- **¼ cup vinegar**
- **1 tbsp sugar**
- **Fresh, flat-leaf parsley, chopped**

1. Peel cucumbers and slice into thin rounds. Sprinkle with salt, and let stand about 10 minutes.

2. Add sliced onions.

3. Mix sour cream, vinegar, and sugar.

4. Pour off liquid from cukes. Add onion.

5. Pour dressing over all, mix and chill.

6. Sprinkle with fresh parsley before serving.

Serves 6-8.

Tip: Use a cheese slicer to thinly slice cucumbers.

Prawn Salad

Although not indigenous to Ukraine, prawns are as popular there as they are in North America. Served with fresh rye bread, this hearty prawn salad makes a wonderful light meal.

- **2 lbs prawns, cooked**

- **1 large lemon, juiced**

- **4 large russet potatoes, cooked and diced**

- **4 large hard-cooked eggs, chopped**

- **1 cup green peas, cooked**

- **1 cup mayonnaise**

- **Salt to taste**

1. Sprinkle prawns with lemon juice.

2. Mix potatoes, chopped eggs and peas with prawns.

3. Season with mayonnaise and salt.

4. Set on a bed of salad greens and chill.

Serves 6-8.

Red Radish Salad

Radishes are rich in sulphur, iron, and iodine, and are a great source of vitamin C with antioxidant and anti-inflammatory properties. They come in several varieties and are generally used as a garnish or salad ingredient because of their mild-to-peppery flavor and unique red-and-white coloration. The earthy-spicy flavor of radish can bring out unexpected flavours in your meals, especially with a buttermilk dressing, as in this Ukrainian recipe.

- **3 bunches red radish, thinly sliced**
- **2 large hard-cooked eggs**
- **1 cup buttermilk**
- **1 tsp icing sugar**
- **1 tbsp vinegar**
- **1 tbsp oil**
- **Salt to taste**
- **Flat leaf parsley for garnish**

1. Slice the eggs in two lengthwise. Scoop out the yolks and mash with salt.

2. Chop egg whites finely and set aside.

3. Combine buttermilk, icing sugar, vinegar, oil and salt. Whisk together in a bowl or shake in a jar until well combined.

4. Arrange radish slices on a platter. Sprinkle with chopped egg whites and drizzle with the buttermilk dressing.

5. Garnish with finely chopped parsley, if desired.

Serves 6.

Sauerkraut Salad

This tasty salad is extremely easy to make, especially if you use store-bought sauerkraut. It's a great make-ahead and goes great with just about any hot or cold dish. You may want to taste the sauerkraut (kapusta) for acidity and, if it's too sour for your liking, rinse in cold water.

- **1 lb sauerkraut, well drained**
- **1 large onion, sliced finely**
- **3 tbsp olive or sunflower oil**
- **2 tsp sugar**
- **Salt & freshly ground pepper**

1. Chop the sauerkraut coarsely and mix with remaining ingredients.

2. Season to taste.

3. Cover and chill several hours before serving.

Serves 6.

Tip: Use cold-pressed (unrefined) oil for best, and most healthful, results. They are available in many supermarkets and most specialty food stores.

Sorrel & Spinach Salad

Sorrel and spinach are very popular in Ukraine, and both grow abundantly there. Sorrel is becoming more common in North American supermarkets, so more of us can enjoy it in unique combinations such as this tangy salad.

- **6 cups tender young sorrel**
- **6 cups baby spinach**
- **5 green onions, finely sliced**
- **2 large hard-cooked eggs, quartered**
- **½ cup olive or sunflower oil**
- **Salt to taste**

1. Coarsely chop sorrel and spinach.

2. Add green onion and eggs. Toss gently.

3. Season with salt and oil.

Serves 10-12.

Tomato Yoghurt Salad

A recently discovered heirloom tomato that is indigenous to Ukraine is called the Black Krim tomato. This chocolate-coloured tomato is a bit of a surprise to the eye. Although it is still not common in supermarkets on this continent, it has captured the imagination of home-growers in North America, so you might find it at farmers' markets in season. Any variety of tomato can be used in this simple but delicious salad – which calls for yoghurt instead of the typical sour cream.

- **5 large ripe tomatoes**
- **1 large sweet onion**
- **½ cup yoghurt**
- **1 tsp icing sugar, sifted**
- **Salt & freshly ground pepper**
- **1 tsp fresh dill, chopped**

1. Cut tomatoes into thick slices.
2. Slice onions into thin rounds.
3. Mix yoghurt and sugar, and season to taste.
4. Arrange tomatoes and onions on a serving plate. Drizzle with the yoghurt dressing and sprinkle with dill.

Serves 8-10.

Tip: Although this recipe calls for yoghurt, you can use sour cream with equally delicious results.

Onion Salad

This unique salad is surprisingly sweet and crunchy, and always a big hit with those fortunate to encounter it. It's well worth making, as on top of being incredibly delicious, it keeps in the fridge indefinitely.

- **2 large sweet onions, thinly sliced**

Brine:
- **1½ cups water**
- **½ cup vinegar**
- **½ cup sugar**
- **1 tbsp salt**

Dressing:
- **½ cup mayonnaise**
- **1 tsp whole celery seed**
- **Salt & freshly ground pepper**

1. Bring the brine ingredients to a boil and pour over onion slices.

2. Allow to marinate in a glass bowl for at least 5 hours, or overnight.

3. Remove onion and cover with the mayonnaise dressing.

4. Toss gently and serve.

Makes about ¾ cup.

Marinated Coleslaw

This sweet and tangy Ukrainian coleslaw goes perfectly with meat dishes like shashlyky (Ukrainian shish kebob), and is a great make-ahead. It will keep for a week in the refrigerator.

- **1 large cabbage, shredded**
- **1 large onion, finely chopped**
- **2 large carrots, grated**
- **2 cups sugar**
- **1 cup vinegar**
- **¾ cup olive or sunflower oil**
- **1 tbsp salt**
- **1 tbsp whole celery seed**

1. Combine vegetables and mix in sugar.
2. Bring vinegar, oil, salt and celery seed to the boiling point.
3. Pour over vegetables. Mix well and chill overnight.
4. Drain excess liquid before serving.

Serves 8-10.

Carpathian Red Cabbage Salad

As well as tasting delicious, cabbage leaves have surprising medicinal uses. In Europe, cabbage is an ancient remedy used to help reduce all types of painful swelling. I found this out when traveling by bus from Kyiv to Bukovina a few years ago. At one point, most of us had swollen ankles, from the heat and sitting for a long time. Our tour guide had the cure. Before going to bed, she had us wrap fresh cabbage leaves around our ankles and slip a sock over them. In the morning, the swelling was gone!

According to the American Medicine Journal from January 1927, cabbage is effective in healing diseases of the eyes, rheumatism, gout, asthma, and ulcers, to name a few disorders. A study conducted in Japan in 1986 discovered that those who consumed the most cabbage had the lowest death rate from all cancers.

Cabbage is low in calories but high in nutrients, rich in Vitamins A, B and C, as well as flavour. It is always readily available in supermarkets, so you can enjoy this tangy red cabbage salad all year.

- **1 small red cabbage**
- **6 cups boiling water**
- **1 large apple, thinly sliced**
- **2 tbsp vinegar**
- **2 tbsp vegetable oil**
- **2 tbsp sugar**
- **¼ tsp salt**

1. Core and shred cabbage. Place in a dutch oven or a large pot.
2. Add 6 cups boiling water and return to the boiling point. Drain.
3. Plunge cabbage into ice water to cool and stop the cooking.
4. Add apple slices to cabbage and toss.
5. Combine vinegar, oil, salt and sugar, and pour over salad.
6. Mix thoroughly and chill before serving.

Serves 4.

Beet and Mushroom Salad

This delicious dish is traditional at Ukrainian Christmas Eve dinners, as it is meatless and dairy-free.

- ½ cup olive oil
- 1 small onion, finely chopped
- 1 cup sliced mushrooms
- 4 cups cooked beets, julienne
- 3 cloves crushed garlic
- 1 tbsp sugar
- 2 tbsp vinegar
- Salt & freshly ground pepper

1. Sauté onion and mushrooms in oil.
2. Add beets and other ingredients. Stir gently.
3. Place in a glass bowl and chill overnight.
4. Serve cold.

Serves 8.

Tip: Cook beets with skins on until tender. Cool, peel, and cut into julienne strips.

Creamy Beet Salad

During the winter, Ukrainians make delicious salads with preserved, cooked, brined, and stored fresh vegetables.

Beets are considered to be one of the powerhouse vegetables, and a favourite for winter salads. These brightly coloured vegetables and their leaves offer not only powerful flavour, but powerful health benefits as well.

This simple but delicious salad is quick and easy to make, and it is a fabulous salad for all seasons.

- **5 medium beets, cooked and diced**
- **2 tbsp butter**
- **½ cup whipping cream**
- **A pinch of salt and freshly ground pepper**
- **1 tsp lemon juice**
- **2 tbsp finely chopped dill**
- **2 tbsp sour cream**

1. Sauté the cooked beets in butter.
2. Add the whipping cream and cook over medium heat for 5 minutes or until the cream is slightly thickened.
3. Season with salt and pepper, and lemon juice.
4. Remove from heat and mix in the dill and sour cream.
5. Chill and serve at room temperature.

Serves 5-6.

Festive Red Cabbage Salad

This colourful salad is a perfect accompaniment to the salted and pickled foods, cheeses, cooked fancy eggs, breads, smoked salmon, caviar, meats and canapés of the holiday season. It's also a nice change from the usual green coleslaw.

As a variation, you can replace the celery seeds with a pinch of caraway seeds—but just a pinch, not a whole teaspoon. More than a pinch of caraway will overpower the salad.

- **1 small red cabbage, finely shredded**
- **1 tbsp salt**
- **1 tsp sugar**
- **1 tbsp vinegar**
- **2 tbsp sunflower oil**
- **1 tsp celery seeds**

1. Scald the cabbage with boiling water, then drain thoroughly.
2. Combine remaining ingredients and pour over cabbage.
3. Toss until well-coated.
4. Chill before serving.

Serves 4-6

Tip: When using sunflower oil in salads, make sure to use unrefined, or cold pressed, oil for the tastiest results. If you can find it, use sunflower oil imported from Ukraine.

Herring and Potato Salad

Herring fillets can usually be purchased from European style delicatessens. Some fish stores stock them too. A herring fillet always means half a herring divided the long way. The best are fillets of Macha style herrings which are mildly salted in rapeseed oil from Poland. I strongly recommend them, especially since they come vacuum packed, already boned and skinned.

For real herring lovers, these fillets are a super fine treat. They can be eaten as is, sliced in pieces with raw onion or with an oil and vinegar dressing as a delicious salad or pickled.

When I was a kid, we used to buy the schmaltz herrings from Iceland, from the barrel at a deli on Hastings St. When we arrived home, Dad and I would sit at the kitchen table, unwrap the herring, slice and devour with rye bread.

We also loved this simple herring and potato salad. You could also add 1 cup cooked diced beets or 1 cup chopped tart apples.

- **6 to 8 prepared herring fillets**

- **2 to 3 cups potatoes, cooked and diced**

- **1 medium onion chopped finely**

- **1 ½ cups thick sour cream, or enough to coat herring and potato**

- **1 or 2 chopped dill pickles**

1. Slice the fillets into one inch pieces.

2. Toss remaining ingredients together gently.

3. Garnish with hard cooked egg slices if desired.

4. Chill before serving with rye bread or crusty style country bread.

Serves 4-6.

Potato Salad with Cooked Sour Cream Dressing

Potatoes are plentiful in Ukraine and are used extensively. A favourite summer salad is potato salad with a cooked sour cream dressing. Radishes are popular in Ukraine as a salad vegetable. They are served as is or added to potato or vegetable salads for texture and flavour. Ukrainians love radishes in their potato salad!

Salad:
- **3 cups diced cooked potatoes**
- **3 tbsp finely chopped green onions**
- **½ c diced celery**
- **½ cup diced cucumber**
- **½ cup sliced radishes**
- **4 hard-cooked eggs, chopped**
- **Salt**
- **½ – ¾ cup sour cream dressing**

Sour cream dressing:
- **1 tbsp flour**
- **½ tsp salt**
- **1 tsp dry mustard**
- **2 tsp sugar**
- **1 egg**
- **3 tbsp vinegar**
- **1 cup sour cream**

1. To make the dressing, mix the dry ingredients. Blend in the egg, cream and vinegar.

2. Cook over medium heat, stirring constantly until mixture thickens.

3. Chill before using.

4. Lightly toss the vegetables with the eggs, add salt to taste and enough salad dressing to moisten.

Serves 6-8.

Red and Green Salad

This simple salad is a creamy delight to the tastebuds. You could add fresh, chopped dill if desired.

- **2 cups radishes, thinly sliced**
- **2 cups cucumbers, sliced**
- **¾ cup green onions, chopped**
- **1 tsp salt**
- **2 tsp sugar**
- **1 cup thick sour cream**

1. Combine the vegetables.
2. Add the sugar and salt to the sour cream, blend well, and pour over the vegetables.
3. Chill well and mix thoroughly before serving.

Serves 4-6.

Tip: Soak radishes in ice cold water to make them extra crisp.

Spring Salad (Ukrainian Style)

Mom always grew leaf lettuce in her fabulous garden. I loved the lettuce because of its unbelievable flavour. However, the washing up was another story! All the little slugs would float to the top of the washing water...ugh! But it was worth the effort.

One of our favourite ways to eat fresh lettuce from the garden was to wrap green onions in lettuce leaves, then dip them into salt before each bite. Delicious!

The sour cream dressing makes this salad! If you are calorie-conscious, try the low-fat or no-fat variety, or mix it with yoghurt. If you can find fresh sour cream without added ingredients, though, and aren't concerned with the few extra calories, you will be in for a fabulous, old-world taste sensation!

- **½ head iceberg lettuce, or leaf lettuce**
- **1 cup sliced radishes**
- **½ cup chopped green onions**
- **½ cup thick sour cream (or yoghurt)**
- **Salt to taste**
- **Tomato wedges**

1. Add sour cream to vegetables and toss together till vegetables are coated.
2. Garnish with tomato wedges.
3. Devour.

Serves 2-4.

Leek and Apple Salad

Leeks look like giant green onions, and they do belong to the onion family. But they have a milder, more delicate, and earthy flavour. The texture of the leek has earned it the nickname "poor man's asparagus." Leeks are very nutritious as well as delicious. Among other things, they are an excellent source of vitamins A, C, K and folate.

To prepare leeks, trim off the dark green tops and root ends, leaving only the white and light green parts. Slice lengthwise and rinse thoroughly under cold water, separating the layers to remove any dirt or sand. If particularly dirty, soak them in cold water for a few minutes, then drain well.

This light and refreshing salad is wonderfully crunchy and full of flavour. As a variation, add some shredded carrots to the mix, and sour cream to the mayo.

- **2 leeks, sliced (white part only)**
- **2 large apples, peeled and grated**
- **Juice and zest of 1 lemon,**
- **1½ tbsp sugar**
- **Salt and pepper to taste**
- **Mayonnaise to coat**

1. Toss the leeks and apples in lemon juice, zest, sugar, salt and pepper.
2. Add enough mayonnaise to lightly coat.
3. Refrigerate for several hours until thoroughly chilled before serving.

Serves about 4.

Peach and Pear Salad

Sweetened fresh fruits, especially with sour or whipped cream, are traditional favourites for dessert in Ukrainian cookery. Fruits that lend themselves particularly well to desserts are plums, apples, pears, cherries, peaches and apricots.

The richness of cream is nicely balanced with fruit, which is low in calories and highly nutritious, making these fruit salads an almost guilt-free option for dessert.

- **4 medium peaches, pitted**
- **3 medium pears, cored**
- **½ cup icing sugar**
- **½ cup walnuts, coarsely chopped**
- **1 tbsp vanilla**
- **½ cup whipping cream**

1. Wash fruit and cut into bite size pieces.
2. Stir in chopped walnuts, sugar and vanilla.
3. Top with whipped cream sweetened to taste.

Serves 4.

Pear and Plum Salad

Ukraine has long been known for its abundance of orchards. It is not uncommon to see fruit trees growing wild along country roads there. Eating pears and making desserts with them always brings back fond memories of when I was in Ukraine and planted a pear seed in the yard of my father's birthplace. This simple but delicious salad is no exception.

- **3 medium pears, cored**
- **8-10 large plums, pitted**
- **½ cup icing sugar**
- **1 fresh lemon, juiced**

1. Cut fruit into bite size pieces.
2. Mix with sugar and lemon juice.

Serves 8.

Sauces & Condiments

Honey Hot Mustard

Any kind of honey can be used for this sauce. Remember that the darker the honey the stronger the flavour, so if you prefer a more robust sauce, use buckwheat honey.

- **½ cup honey**
- **¼ cup dry mustard**
- **1 tbsp flour**
- **2 large eggs**
- **⅓ cup vinegar**

1. Combine all ingredients.
2. Whisk until smooth.
3. Cook over medium heat until thick (about 5 minutes), stirring constantly.
4. Serve over vegetables, eggs, meats or as a dipping sauce.

Makes 1 cup.

Hot Mustard and Sour Cream Sauce

This tangy sauce is very versatile and delicious. Drizzle it over cabbage rolls, potato pancakes, meat patties, any kind of roasted meat, roast beef or pork sandwiches. Delicious in a bowl of borshch!

- **4 tsp butter**
- **4 tsp flour**
- **1 cup sour cream**
- **2 eggs**
- **¼ tsp salt**
- **2 tsp prepared hot mustard**

1. Melt butter over medium heat. Add flour and blend.

2. Beat sour cream with eggs and salt, and add to butter mixture.

3. Cook, stirring until sauce is very hot, but not boiling.

4. Remove from heat and mix in mustard.

5. Cover and refrigerate for a few hours before serving.

Makes 1 ½ cups.

Cucumber Sauce

The popularity of cucumber, fresh or pickled, is immense—especially in Germanic and Slavic countries, where it may be considered, besides beets and cabbage, the national vegetable. And in many parts of Europe and North America, cosmetic products made from cucumbers are highly thought of as beautifiers.

This refreshing cucumber sauce can be served in lettuce cups or drizzled over any meat or fish, baked potatoes or grilled vegetables.

- **1 large field (or English) cucumber, peeled**
- **1-2 tbsp chopped green onion**
- **2 tbsp vinegar**
- **¼ tsp salt**
- **A pinch of pepper**
- **⅔ cup sour cream**

1. Pare and chop the cucumber finely or whiz in a food processor.
2. Drain off any excess liquid over a sieve.
3. Combine the cucumber with the remaining ingredients.

Makes about 2 cups.

Horseradish Mayonnaise

This Ukrainian mayonnaise adds a tangy zest to European hot dogs and roast beef sandwiches, and is wonderful on a wedge of crisp iceberg lettuce.

- **4 large hard-cooked eggs**
- **1 tbsp icing sugar**
- **2 tbsp freshly squeezed lemon juice**
- **1½ tsp dry mustard**
- **1 cup sour cream**
- **2 tbsp mayonnaise**
- **¼ cup horseradish, finely grated**

1. Halve eggs and separate whites from yolks.

2. Finely chop egg whites; set aside.

3. In medium bowl, mash egg yolks. Add in sugar, lemon juice, mustard, sour cream, and mayonnaise.

4. Stir in horseradish and egg whites.

5. Store in an airtight container. Keeps up to 4 days in the refrigerator.

Makes about 2 cups.

Tip: Fresh grated horseradish is best, if you can find it. If not, use prepared (not creamy) horseradish.

Dill Mayonnaise

Many Ukrainian dishes are prepared with mayonnaise and/or dill. But together, this combination is a winner!

This rich and creamy dill mayonnaise is delicious and versatile. It enhances the flavour of fish, poultry, eggs and salads. It can be used to marinate meats, and makes a zesty, tasty sandwich spread.

I love it as a dip with appetizers such as miniature chicken or salmon croquettes, or cocktail meatballs. Great with veggies, too!

- **1 ½ cups mayonnaise, preferably homemade**
- **1 cup chopped dill**
- **1 clove garlic, finely minced**
- **2 tbsp capers, drained**
- **2 tbsp fresh lemon juice**
- **2 tbsp sour cream**

1. Process all the ingredients in a food processor until well blended, for about four seconds.

2. Enjoy!

Makes 2 cups.

Decadent Dill Sauce

This traditional and very simple sauce is delicious served over steamed carrots, boiled new (or baked) potatoes, or salmon. It also adds a special touch to cabbage rolls.

- **1 medium onion, finely chopped**

- **2 tbsp fresh dill, chopped**

- **4 tbsp butter**

- **2 cups whipping cream**

1. Fry onions and dill in butter over low-medium heat until the onion is tender.

2. Add the whipping cream, and simmer for about 15 minutes.

Yield: about 3 cups.

Dill Cream Sauce

This sauce is lovely with baked salmon or boiled new potatoes.

- **3 tbsp butter**
- **4 tbsp flour**
- **¾ cup milk**
- **¾ cup cream**
- **Salt to taste**
- **3 tbsp dill, finely chopped**

1. Over medium low heat, blend flour into melted butter.

2. Add milk and cream, bring to a boil, stirring constantly.

3. Season to taste. Cook for 5 minutes, and add the dill.

4. Simmer 15 minutes, stirring occasionally, until thickened.

Makes about 2 cups.

Easter Beets & Horseradish

The mildness of beets balances the bite of the horseradish in this traditional Easter relish, which some connoisseurs refer to as the caviar of all relishes. Keeps well in refrigerator for up to a week. Freezes well.

- **10 cups cooked beets, grated**
- **2 cups ground horseradish**
- **4 cups white vinegar**
- **4 cups sugar**
- **4 tsp salt**

1. In a saucepan, combine salt, vinegar and sugar; bring to a boil.

2. Add to beets and horseradish and mix well.

3. Taste and if desired, adjust vinegar, sugar or salt. Should be on the piquant side.

4. Fill sterilized jars with relish and refrigerate.

Makes 14 cups.

Easter Horseradish

Zesty horseradish is a traditional accompaniment for Easter meats such as ham, sausage, pork, and duck. While it's traditional at Easter it can, of course, be enjoyed on any occasion!

- **1 cup ground horseradish**
- **1 tbsp butter, softened**
- **¼ cup liquid honey**
- **10 eggs hard-cooked**

1. Mix horseradish, butter and honey until smooth.

2. Mash eggs with a fork (or process until fine, or put through a fine sieve).

3. Add to the horseradish mixture.

4. Mix well.

Makes about 3 cups.

Horseradish Sauce

Horseradish is grown for its pungent roots, which are generally grated, mixed with vinegar and salt, and used as a condiment or relish. One tablespoon of horseradish has only 2 calories, is low in sodium, and provides dietary fiber. Although it is not clear where horseradish originates, some scholars believe it is indigenous to Eastern Europe. A traditional Ukrainian Easter condiment, it can be enjoyed any time of year.

- **6 tbsp grated fresh horseradish**
- **2 cups sour cream**
- **2 tsp salt**
- **2 tbsp sugar**
- **2 tbsp vinegar**

1. Mix all ingredients in a glass bowl.
2. Adjust seasonings to taste.
3. Let stand at room temperature for 1 hour before serving so flavours can develop.

Makes about 3 cups.

Mushroom Powder

Dried mushrooms of wild species are highly prized by connoisseurs because they are exceptionally rich in flavour and aroma.

There is no taste quite like that of cooked dried wild mushrooms. A few of them will change a commonplace dish into a gourmet specialty!

In Ukraine, traditionally and even today, wild mushroom-picking is a family activity. When I was in Ukraine some years ago, I saw many families doing just that. One day while touring through the Carpathian Mountains, we saw families along the roadside selling baskets full of freshly-picked mushrooms. We bought several (the beautiful hand-made baskets were not, unfortunately, for sale). Then we stopped at the first restaurant we saw, a delightful establishment called The Sunflower, where the chef cooked them in cream for us. What an unbelievably delicious and delectable taste sensation!

I realize that few people ever encounter such good fortune as I did that day, but dried mushrooms can mimic that delectable taste. They are readily available in supermarkets. You can even find wild ones occasionally, although species like morels (Paulette's favourite) are very expensive.

Dried mushroom powder makes it easy to add mushroom flavour to whatever you are cooking. It's also a good substitute for fresh mushrooms when you have none on hand

Here's how to make your own mushroom powder. It's easy! You can process store-bought dried mushrooms into a fine powder in your food processor, grind them with a mikitra (mortar and pestle), or just place them in a sturdy cloth bag and pound them with a rolling pin or similarly heavy, blunt object. Sift the powder through a fine sieve (or skip this stage if you like little chunks) and store in an airtight container.

One teaspoon of mushroom powder adds the equivalent taste of about half a cup of fresh mushrooms.

Mushroom Sauce

This savoury sauce is ideal over stuffed eggs, boiled or baked potatoes, chicken, meat, fish, and even just toast.

- **½ small onion, finely chopped**
- **2 tbsp butter**
- **1 cup mushrooms, sliced**
- **1 tbsp flour**
- **½ cup stock, or water**
- **½ cup sour cream**
- **1 tsp chopped dill or flat-leaf parsley**
- **Salt & freshly ground pepper**

1. Sauté the onion in butter until soft.
2. Add the mushrooms and cook for about 10 minutes.
3. Sprinkle with the flour and mix.
4. Poor in the stock, or water, and stir constantly until smooth and thick.
5. Add the sour cream and cook another minute.
6. Mix in the dill or parsley and season to taste.

Makes about 2 cups.

Creamy Mushroom Gravy

Mushroom gravy is one of the world's top taste sensations, and perennially popular with Ukrainians around the world. If you haven't made it, try it and you will see why!

- **3 cups white or brown mushrooms, sliced**
- **2 tbsp oil**
- **2 tbsp butter**
- **2 tbsp flour**
- **½ cup stock or water**
- **1 cup whipping or sour cream**
- **Salt & freshly ground pepper**

1. Sauté sliced mushrooms in oil.

2. In a heavy skillet, melt butter and stir in flour. Cook until golden.

3. Add stock and mushrooms, stirring until gravy thickens.

4. Add cream and season to taste.

Makes about 3 cups.

Tip: If you are counting calories or fat grams, you can use a lighter cream, but the flavour will be less intense.

Mushroom Gravy with Browned Flour

Browned flour gives gravy a nice robust flavour without using meat stock or drippings. To brown flour, all you do is heat a medium cast iron frying pan over medium heat until hot, but not smoking. Add 1-2 cups of white flour, and stir frequently with a wooden spoon until the flour begins to colour. Then stir constantly until the flour turns a deep golden brown. This gravy is traditional for Sviat Vechir, the traditional Ukrainian Christmas Eve dinner of 12 meatless dishes, but is delicious any time of year. I may be biased, but my mom's recipe for this gravy was, in my opinion, the absolute best.

- **1 small onion, finely chopped**
- **6 tbsp oil**
- **1 large clove garlic, crushed**
- **4 tbsp browned flour**
- **4 cups hot water**
- **3 cups fresh mushrooms, sliced**
- **1 tsp salt**
- **Freshly ground black pepper**

1. Sauté onion in oil until tender.
2. Stir in garlic, and cook for a minute.
3. Sprinkle browned flour over onion and stir. Add hot water and mushrooms, season to taste with salt and pepper.
4. Simmer 15 minutes, stirring occasionally, until thickened.

Makes about 4 cups.

Tip: Browned flour has about half the thickening power of white flour, so double it up in recipes calling for white flour.

Povydlo (Plum Butter)

Mom used to make a beautiful thick plum jam called povydlo. It's actually more like a plum butter. She would slowly cook the fruit pulp in the oven for hours. She used it as a filling for pastries, or just eaten like jam. If you have access to a lot of prune plums (also called Italian plums), try making povydlo – you'll be glad you did!

Please note, you need prune plums for this. All prunes are dried plums, but not all plums can become prunes. In order to become a prune, a plum must be capable of drying with its pit in place. Most plums will ferment at the pit. The plum destined to become a prune plum stays on the tree until fully ripe in order to develop enough sugar. The plum also must have a freestone pit.

Use fully ripe prune plums that are beginning to form wrinkles at the stems. At this stage, the plums are sweetest and also less juicy. Wash, pit and quarter the plums. Place them in a large roaster and add a small amount of water to prevent burning.

Cook for about 2 hours at 350°F, stirring from time to time, until fairly thick. Sweeten fruit to taste and add spices or flavouring if desired, and keep cooking, probably for 5-6 hours or longer, until good and thick. You should almost be able to stand a spoon in it upright. But keep an eye on it so it doesn't burn.

Pack into hot sealers and cover. Povydlo is well concentrated and requires no sealing, but if you wish you may do so in a hot water bath.

Breads & Quick Breads

Beetniks

These beet leaf-wrapped bread rolls are a delectable traditional treat! In the "old days" we used to call them beet leaf holubtsi, but more recently they have come to be known as "beetniks." They're quite easy to make, especially if you use frozen bread dough, make the dough in your bread maker, or buy bread dough from your favourite bakery. Serve beetniks warm with salted sweet cream, or sour cream mixed with finely chopped onion and fresh dill.

- **2 lbs bread dough (enough for 2 loaves)**
- **3 dozen beet leaves, medium to large**
- **Melted butter**
- **Salt**

1. Generously butter a large casserole dish or medium size roaster.

2. Wash beet leaves and trim any tough stems. Put leaves in a warm oven until pliable, or scald with boiling water. Pat dry.

3. Take a piece of dough the size of a walnut, roll into a ball and wrap it loosely in a beet leaf, like a cabbage roll.

4. Arrange the rolls in layers, sprinkling each layer with melted butter and salt. Only fill to half-full.

5. Top with a layer of leaves, brush with melted butter, cover, and let rise in a warm place until double in bulk.

6. Bake, uncovered, in a preheated 350°F oven for one hour.

Makes 2-3 dozen.

Tip: If you're using frozen dough, wrap it in the leaves while it's still cold, before it rises.

Country Kitchen Grain Bread

Since ancient times bread has held a special, primary position in the cuisine of the Ukrainian people. In ancient times, the grain for flour was ground manually between two rounded grindstones. In the 13th century, water mills and windmills appeared, and flour milling in Ukraine soon became highly developed. Rye bread has long been a Ukrainian staple. This recipe is a North American adaptation, using a combination of whole wheat and rye flour.

- **2 tbsp active dry yeast**
- **½ cup honey**
- **⅓ cup shortening**
- **3 cups lukewarm water**
- **5 cups sifted all-purpose flour, divided**
- **1½ cups whole wheat flour**
- **1½ cups rye flour**
- **½ cup cornmeal**
- **¾ cup skim milk powder**

1. In a large mixing bowl, dissolve yeast, honey and shortening in lukewarm water. Let stand for 10 minutes.

2. Add 2 cups all-purpose flour and remaining ingredients in order given. Stir thoroughly between each addition.

3. Cover and let rise until doubled in bulk. Punch dough down, turn out onto floured surface.

4. Knead in as much of the remaining all-purpose flour as needed to make a firm, smooth dough. Knead well and shape into 3 loaves.

5. Put into greased pans and let rise until doubled.

6. Bake at 400°F for 20 minutes. Reduce heat to 350°F and bake 20-40 minutes more, or until done. (Loaf should sound hollow when tapped.)

7. Brush with butter while warm.

Makes 3 loaves.

Old Country Rye Bread

Ukraine is known as the "breadbasket of Europe," because its fertile black earth has been ideal for cultivating grains for millennia.

The famous French novelist Honoré de Balzac, who lived in Ukraine in the 1840s, noted 77 ways of preparing bread. This is certainly a testament to the Ukrainian people's culinary creativity!

Ukrainians have a special fondness for rye bread. This one is easy to make and wickedly delicious.

- **3 cups all purpose flour**
- **2 tbsp active dry yeast**
- **1 tbsp caraway seeds**
- **2 cups water**
- **⅓ cup molasses**
- **2 tbsp butter**
- **1 tbsp sugar**
- **1 tbsp salt**
- **3–3 ½ cups rye flour**

1. In a large bowl, mix the white flour, yeast, and caraway seeds.

2. In a saucepan over medium low heat, warm the water, molasses, butter, sugar, and salt, stirring to blend.

3. Add this mixture to the dry ingredients.

4. Beat with an electric mixer at a low speed for a minute. Then on high speed for three minutes.

5. Add enough rye flour by hand to make a soft dough and knead until smooth.

6. Cover and rest for 20 minutes. Punch down the dough and divide in half. Shape each piece into a round ball and place on a greased baking tray.

7. Cut two to three slashes across the top of dough with a sharp knife or razor blade. Let rise until double in size. Brush with water for a crusty top.

8. Bake at 400°F for 30 minutes, or until done. Loaf should sound hollow when tapped.

Makes 2 loaves.

Dill Bread Express

Dill is one of my favorite herbs. You could say I have a violent passion for dill! It is divine with potatoes, in dips and salad dressings, and in egg, chicken and fish dishes. It's always best to use fresh dill for an authentic dill flavour. Luckily, fresh dill is now available year-round in most supermarkets and green grocers.

This recipe for Dill Bread Express makes a nice change from garlic bread. It's a great make-ahead and freezes well.

- **1 loaf of French bread, cut in half lengthwise**

- **½ cup soft butter**

- **2 tbsp fresh, finely chopped dill**

1. Mix the dill with the butter and generously spread on both halves.

2. Put sides together and wrap in foil. Bake at 400°F for about 15 minutes.

3. Serve warm.

Makes 1 loaf.

Pampushky (Garlic Puffs)

Pampushky are delightful yeast treats that come in both savory and sweet variations, either baked or deep fried. They are a fantastic freezer-friendly make-ahead and a great hit at parties!

This recipe is very adaptable. For a sweet variation, fill with jam or sprinkle with icing sugar and cinnamon.

You can also use this dough to make baked pampushky. Make basic buns, and before baking brush tops with a mixture of beaten egg and water. After baking, brush with a mixture of oil, minced garlic, salt and chopped fresh dill. Or for a sweet variation, brush tops with honey and sprinkle with powdered sugar and cinnamon.

- **1 cup warm water**
- **1 tbsp active dry yeast**
- **2 tbsp sugar**
- **3 cups flour**
- **1 tsp salt**
- **2 tbsp oil**
- **3 cloves garlic, mashed with salt**
- **Oil for frying**

1. Mix yeast, sugar and water and allow to foam.

2. Knead together flour, salt, oil and yeast mixture to form a soft dough.

3. Place dough in an oiled bowl, turn to cover with oil, and cover bowl with plastic wrap. Let rise until doubled in bulk and punch down.

4. Take small pieces of dough, roll each between lightly oiled palms into 1-inch balls, and set on a floured towel.

5. Shallow-fry dough balls in a skillet in 2 inches of hot oil (375°F) on all sides until golden. Do not overcrowd.

6. Remove with a slotted spoon and drain on paper towels.

7. Roll in mashed garlic, or sprinkle with garlic salt.

Makes several dozen.

Bread Clouds

Every kitchen should turn into a bakery from time to time! It's exciting to make real bread with yeast. Magic happens when you feel the dough become elastic under your hands. And smelling the aroma of bread baking is very special indeed!

When I was a kid my sister and I used to do something unique when mom's brown bread came out of the oven. We used to slice it hot (which really is a no-no) and eat the bread with slices of fresh apple from our own apple tree. I don't remember how that really came about or why—and you have to admit that it is unusual—but the flavor combination was unbelievably delicious.

Mom also made these wonderful light and airy buns that we called "white balls of fluff" or simply bread clouds. These buns can also be baked in greased round or rectangular pans. They are great served warm with butter and strawberry preserves—or sliced fresh apples.

- **1 cup warm water**
- **1 tbsp active dry yeast**
- **1 tbsp sugar**
- **1 cup milk, scalded**
- **4 tbsp butter**
- **4 tbsp sugar**
- **1 ½ tsp salt**
- **2 large eggs, well beaten**
- **4 cups flour**

1. In a mixing bowl, combine the warm water, sugar and yeast to dissolve. Set aside until foamy.

2. Melt the butter in the hot milk, then cool.

3. When cooled, mix in the sugar, salt and well beaten eggs. Pour into the yeast mixture. Add the flour, and beat thoroughly to form a thin batter.

4. Let rise for about 1¼ hours.

5. Spoon the risen dough into buttered deep muffin tins half full. Let rise for another ½ hour.

6. Preheat oven to 400°F and bake for 15 minutes or until golden.

Makes 30 buns.

Golden Honey Wheat Bread

Honey is an excellent sweetener for bread, as it improves both the flavour and the keeping quality. Here's a mouth-watering quick bread to satisfy your sweet tooth. Great for the festive season, or any time!

- **2½ cups whole wheat flour**
- **1 tsp baking soda**
- **½ tsp salt**
- **1 tsp baking powder**
- **¼ tsp cinnamon**
- **½ cup light honey**
- **¼ cup oil**
- **1½ cups buttermilk**
- **1 tbsp orange zest**
- **½ cup chopped walnuts**
- **½ cup chopped raisins**

1. In a large bowl beat together all ingredients, except walnuts and raisins.

2. When well blended, mix in walnuts and raisins.

3. Pour batter into a well-greased and floured large loaf pan. Let rest for 20 minutes.

4. Bake at 375°F for 50-60 minutes. Cool on rack before devouring.

Makes one loaf.

Quick Sweet Rye Bread

Quick breads are so named because they rise with baking powder or soda as they bake and so are much quicker to make than yeast breads. This recipe for quick sweet rye bread is wonderful at breakfast with butter and honey or jam, or as a mid morning snack.

- ½ cup water
- ½ cup sugar
- ½ cup brown sugar
- 1 tbsp honey
- 1 tsp baking soda
- 1 large egg, beaten
- 4-5 cups rye flour

1. In a small saucepan, boil the water, sugars and honey together for 3-4 minutes, then cool.

2. Mix in the egg and soda.

3. Place the flour in a large bowl and form a well in the centre.

4. Pour the liquid into the well and work the flour in.

5. Knead the dough until smooth.

6. Divide in two and place each half into a well-buttered loaf pan.

7. Bake at 350°F for 40 minutes. Rest 15 minutes before serving.

Makes 2 loaves.

Buckwheat Turnover

This traditional treat is easy to make with a food processor. It's a great make-ahead – the dough and filling keep well refrigerated for a couple of days. Delicious with sour cream or yoghurt.

Dough:
- **2 cups flour**
- **1 tsp salt**
- **½ cup butter**
- **1 large egg, beaten**
- **¼ cup ice water**
- **2 tbsp cornmeal**

Filling:
- **½ cup roasted buckwheat groats**
- **1 cup hot water**
- **1 tsp salt**
- **6 strips double smoked bacon**
- **2 tbsp oil**
- **1 med onion, finely chopped**
- **1 tsp freshly ground pepper**

Glaze:
- **1 large egg white, beaten**
- **1 tsp water**

1. Combine flour, salt and butter in processor bowl and pulse a few times until mealy. With machine running, add beaten egg and water, and mix until dough forms a ball. Let rest 2 hours.

2. Add water and salt to the buckwheat groats. Cover and cook 20 minutes until fluffy.

3. Fry bacon until crisp. Remove from pan, add onion and sauté until soft. Add buckwheat, bacon and pepper. Taste and adjust seasoning.

4. Roll out dough on a lightly floured work surface into a rectangle ¼ inch thick. Cover one half with cooled filling, leaving a 1-inch border.

5. Fold the other half over filled side and press edges with a fork to seal.

6. Place on a baking sheet sprinkled with cornmeal.

7. Bake in preheated 375°F oven for 30 minutes. Brush with glaze and bake 8 to 10 minutes more.

Serves 12.

Buckwheat Pancakes

With their lovely nutty flavour, these buckwheat pancakes (hrechanyky in Ukrainian) are a traditional Ukrainian old-world accompaniment to borshch. Buckwheat flour is readily available across North America in gourmet food shops, European delis and even some upscale supermarkets.

- **2 tbsps active dry yeast**
- **1 tbsp honey**
- **½ cup milk, scalded and cooled to lukewarm**
- **1 cup buttermilk**
- **2 large eggs, beaten**
- **2 tbsp oil or melted butter**
- **1½ cups buckwheat flour**
- **1 tsp salt**

1. Dissolve yeast and honey in lukewarm milk. Let stand 10 minutes.

2. Stir in buttermilk, eggs, oil or butter.

3. Beat in flour and salt until smooth. Cover, let stand 30 minutes or more.

4. Stir down, rest 10 minutes. Batter should be thin.

5. Cook as for regular pancakes in a hot greased heavy frying pan.

6. Serve with butter and thick sour cream.

Serves 4.

Tip: For 1 cup buttermilk substitute 1 cup plain yoghurt or add enough milk to 1 tablespoon of lemon juice (or vinegar) to make 1 cup. Let stand 5 minutes.

Traditional Baked Pyrohy

Fillings for this stuffed bread, called pyrih (singular) or pyrohy (plural) in Ukrainian, are limitless. They can range from sweet ones like jams or thick fruit preserves to savoury ones of mushrooms, meat, sauerkraut, or mashed potato with dill.

- **1 tsp sugar**
- **¼ cup lukewarm water**
- **1 tbsp active dry yeast**
- **1 cup scalded milk**
- **¼ cup butter**
- **2 large eggs, beaten**
- **2 tsp salt**
- **1 tbsp sugar**
- **4-5 cups sifted flour**

1. Scald milk, add butter, cool to lukewarm. Dissolve sugar in water, sprinkle with yeast, let stand 10 minutes.

2. Add eggs, salt, sugar and yeast to milk. Add in enough flour to make a medium soft dough. Knead until smooth. Place in a bowl, cover, and let rise until doubled. Punch down, knead a few times in bowl, and allow to rise again.

3. Roll dough ¼ inch thick and cut into 2 rectangles. Place one rectangle on a greased baking sheet and spread with filling. Cover with other rectangle and seal edges securely. Prick top in several places.

4. For individual pyrohy, roll dough ¼ inch thick, and cut into squares. Place some filling in the center of each square. Fold over to make a triangle. Seal edges well. Cover and let rise in a warm place about half an hour.

5. Brush with melted butter, and bake at 375°F for 30-35 minutes, or until crust is golden.

6. Serve warm, with a sweet or savory sauce of your choice.

Serves 12.

Nalysnyky (Crepes)

One of Ukraine's national specialties is nalysnyky – paper-thin pancakes that resemble French crepes. They can be rolled, folded or layered, and are an unbelievably delectable treat. A savoury cottage cheese filling is traditional, but fillings can be sweet as well as savoury.

- **3 large eggs**
- **2 cups milk**
- **1½ cups flour**
- **¼ tsp baking powder**
- **½ tsp salt**

1. Beat eggs, add milk and continue beating until mixed.

2. Sift flour, baking powder and salt. Add to the milk mixture, beating until smooth.

3. Fry in a hot 9-inch non-stick crepe pan. If using a regular skillet, brush lightly with oil each time.

4. Pour about ¼ cup batter into the hot pan, just enough to thinly coat the bottom. Tilt the pan back and forth quickly to spread the batter evenly. The edges will curl and when the entire top is dry, turn over. The underside should be golden brown. The second side takes only seconds to turn colour.

5. Turn out onto a plate. Spread the lighter side with the filling of your choice and roll up. Place in a shallow pan and keep warm in 200°F oven.

6. Continue until batter is all used.

7. Serve warm.

Makes about 2 dozen.

Cottage Cheese Filling for Nalysnyky

A traditional favourite, and still one of the most popular amongst Ukrainians. Crepe connoisseurs of all backgrounds also appreciate its delicately delicious flavour and versatility. Topped with fruit preserves, it can be a sweet. Or, for a savoury dish, top with your favourite sauce or add chopped dill and/or other herbs to the cottage cheese. There are no rules other than to savour and enjoy.

- **2 cups creamed cottage cheese, well-drained**
- **1 egg yolk**
- **1 tbsp heavy cream**
- **2 tbsp sugar**
- **1 tsp lemon zest**

1. Mash cottage cheese.
2. Add remaining ingredients and mix thoroughly.
3. Spread one tablespoon or more of filling on each crepe and roll.

Makes just over 2 cups filling.

Mushroom Filling for Nalysnyky

For an extra special, old world taste sensation, use wild mushrooms or a combination of wild and cultivated fresh mushrooms.

- **2 cups fresh mushrooms, chopped**
- **½ cup onion, finely chopped**
- **3 tbsp butter**
- **1 tsp salt, or to taste**
- **1 large egg, slightly beaten**
- **Freshly ground black pepper**

1. Stir-fry mushrooms and onions in butter until onion is soft. Cool.
2. Add egg, salt and pepper.
3. Spread one tablespoon or more of filling on each crepe and roll.

Makes just over 2 cups of filling.

Poppy Seed Roll

This traditional poppy seed roll (makivnyk) is a favourite traditional Ukrainian Christmas dessert that is delicious any time of year.

- **2 tbsp active dry yeast**
- **½ cup lukewarm water**
- **2 tsp sugar**
- **1 cup scalded milk, cooled to lukewarm**
- **5 cups flour, divided**
- **½ cup butter**
- **8 tbsp sugar**
- **2 large eggs**
- **2 egg yolks**
- **1 tsp vanilla**
- **1½ tsp grated lemon rind**
- **1 tsp salt**
- **Poppy seed filling**

1. Dissolve sugar in lukewarm water. Add yeast and let stand 10 minutes in a warm place. Combine with milk and 1 cup flour and let rise until bubbles appear (30-45 minutes).

2. Beat sugar and butter until light. Set aside. Beat eggs and egg yolks until light and foamy. Add salt. Combine eggs and butter mixture and fold into yeast sponge. Add lemon rind and vanilla. Add remaining flour and knead 10 minutes. Cover and let rise until double.

3. Punch down and let rise again. Divide dough into 3 balls. Roll each ball into a rectangular shape about ½ inch thick. Brush a stiffly beaten egg white on the rectangle, not quite reaching the edges. (This is to prevent filling from separating the dough.) Spread filling over the egg white. Roll like a jelly roll and seal edges. Place in a greased pan, cover, and let rise in a warm place until double.

4. Bake at 350°F for 15 minutes, lower temperature to 300°F and bake 40 minutes more. Brush with 1 tablespoon brown sugar dissolved in 2 tablespoons hot water. Cool completely before cutting.

Makes 3 rolls.

Poppy Seed Filling

My mom used poppy seeds in many wonderful desserts. I learned from her that you should never just throw the poppy seeds dry into a recipe.

To get the true, full favour of the poppy seed, you must first soak then grind the poppy seeds. Mom used to grind them until they became milky in a special little grinder that I have never seen anywhere since it broke years ago. A coffee grinder, blender or even just a rolling pin will do the trick.

This filling for Ukrainian poppy seed roll can be used with equally delicious results in strudel as well as dessert perogies. For dessert perogies, prepare as for savoury perogies, using regular perogy dough and cooking method. Serve with sour cream or sweetened whipped cream.

- **1 cup poppy seeds**

- **⅓ cup honey or sugar**

- **½ cup ground walnuts or almonds**

- **1 egg white, stiffly beaten**

- **1 tsp grated lemon rind**

1. Scald poppy seeds in boiling water. Drain.

2. Cover with warm water and let sit for 30 minutes. Drain thoroughly in a fine sieve.

3. Grind poppy seeds with a fine blade of a food chopper or nut grinder. (You can also use a blender, coffee grinder, mortar, or rolling pin.)

4. Mix sugar or honey, lemon rind, nuts, and stiffly-beaten egg white. Mix gently into poppy seeds.

Makes about 2 cups.

Tip: If you're lucky and can find one, use a makitra, which is a ceramic bowl that has ridges inside it, like a mortar and pestle.

Puffy Pampushky

Every country has their version of this puffy, light and tender choux pastry. In Ukrainian cuisine, they make a delectable soup accompaniment or dessert. For the soup accompaniment they're fried in very tiny puffs. For dessert, the balls are larger and are served floating in chocolate or fruit sauce. These are delightful, and not at all difficult to make.

- **½ cup water**
- **¼ cup butter**
- **Pinch salt**
- **½ cup flour**
- **3 large eggs**
- **1 tbsp rum or brandy**

1. Bring the water, butter and salt to a boil.

2. Add the flour, all at once, stirring quickly with a wooden spoon until the mixture leaves the sides of the pot.

3. Remove from the stove, cool slightly.

4. Add the eggs, one at a time, and beat with an electric mixer or by hand really well. Add the rum or brandy.

5. Drop the batter from a teaspoon into hot fat (350°F) and fry until golden. Be careful not to crowd.

6. Drain on paper towels. Sprinkle with icing sugar and serve hot, or with a sauce of your choice.

Serves 8.

Tip: For a superb fruit sauce that's super easy to make, just whiz sugared fruit, fresh or frozen, in a food processor until creamy and smooth.

Sour Cream Crescents

These delightful dainties will melt in your mouth! This recipe calls for a walnut filling, but for a nice variation use thick apricot preserves, or try any of your other favourite fillings.

- **1 tbsp active dry yeast**
- **½ cup lukewarm water**
- **1 cup butter**
- **1 tsp salt**
- **4 cups flour**
- **3 large eggs, beaten**
- **1 tsp lemon zest**
- **1 cup sour cream**
- **1 tsp vanilla**
- **1¾ cups sugar**

Walnut Filling:
- **2 cups ground walnuts**
- **½ cup sugar**
- **2 egg whites**
- **1 tsp lemon juice**

1. Dissolve yeast in ½ cup lukewarm water.

2. In a large bowl, mix the butter with the flour and salt until mealy.

3. Add yeast mixture, sour cream, eggs, vanilla and lemon zest.

4. Mix dough well. Keep covered with plastic wrap for two hours, or overnight in the refrigerator.

5. Combine the ground walnuts, sugar, egg whites and lemon juice to create the filling.

6. Roll out dough on a sugared or lightly floured pastry board, in a circle or rectangular shape.

7. Spread with filling. Cut in wedges (triangles) and roll, wide side to narrow. Curve into crescent shapes.

8. Put on a parchment-lined and greased baking sheet and let rise till double.

9. Bake at 400°F for about 15 minutes, depending on the size of the twists, until golden.

Makes 16 crescents.

Sylvia's Christmas Honey Bread

This is a quick Christmas honey bread (called medivnyk in Ukrainian) recipe that you can make ahead and store for a few weeks. It's usually made with buckwheat honey, which imparts intense flavour and a rich dark color. Many types of honey are available, each with its own special flavour. Choose the one you like best.

- **2½ cups liquid honey**
- **8 large eggs, separated**
- **½ cup butter, softened**
- **2 cups sugar**
- **6 cups flour**
- **2 tsp baking soda**
- **2 tsp baking powder**
- **1 tbsp cinnamon**
- **1 tsp freshly grated nutmeg**
- **1 whole orange, juice and zest**
- **1 cup strong black coffee**
- **1 cup sour cream**
- **1 cup finely chopped walnuts, optional**

1. Beat egg yolks and butter until light and fluffy.

2. Add in the honey and sugar to the butter mixture, and continue beating.

3. Sift dry ingredients and add to honey mixture. Mix in the orange juice and zest, coffee, and sour cream.

4. Beat egg whites until stiff peaks form, and fold into batter, a little at a time.

5. Stir in the nuts.

6. Pour into 2 well-greased and floured large loaf pans.

7. Bake at 325°F for one hour.

8. Cool on a rack. Wrap loaves in aluminum foil if you're planning to store them for any length of time.

Makes 2 loaves.

Pumpkin Babka

Mashed pumpkin imparts a mellow, yellow colour to babka (Ukrainian Easter bread) and keeps it fresh and soft for days. It also reduces the number of eggs needed. This is a very old recipe.

- **2 tsp sugar**
- **½ cup lukewarm water**
- **2 tbsp active dry yeast**
- **1 cup scalded milk, cooled to lukewarm**
- **1 cup flour**
- **6 large eggs**
- **1 tsp salt**
- **1 cup sugar**
- **2 tsp vanilla**
- **½ cup orange juice**
- **1 cup butter, melted**
- **⅔ cup mashed cooked pumpkin, or canned**
- **2 tbsp grated lemon rind**
- **6 cups all purpose flour, or more**
- **1 cup seedless raisins**

1. Dissolve sugar in lukewarm water, sprinkle yeast over it and let stand 10 minutes. Add milk and 1 cup flour. Beat well. Cover. Let rise until bubbly.

2. Beat eggs with salt, add sugar slowly, then the orange juice and vanilla, beating constantly. Mix in pumpkin, lemon rind and melted butter. Add to yeast mixture. Stir in flour, 2 cups at a time, adding more as needed to make a soft dough. Knead for 8-10 minutes.

3. Add raisins, kneading until well distributed. Cover and let rise in a warm place until double in bulk.

4. Punch down, knead a few times and let rise again. Generously butter tall, round baking pans, or large juice cans and fill one-third full.

5. Cover and let rise in a warm place until dough reaches the top of the tin. Bake at 400°F for 15 minutes, then lower to 350°F and continue baking 40 minutes. When tapped on the top, it should make a hollow sound. Carefully remove the loaves from the pans and cool, on pillows if desired.

Makes 3 loaves.

Easter Babka

- **2 tbsp active dry yeast**
- **1 tsp sugar**
- **1 cup warm water**
- **2 cups scalded milk, divided**
- **9 cups flour, divided**
- **10 egg yolks**
- **1 cup sugar**
- **1 tsp salt**
- **½ lb butter, melted**
- **1 tbsp orange rind, grated**
- **5 egg whites, stiffly beaten**
- **1 cup golden raisins**

1. Combine first 3 ingredients, mixing until yeast is dissolved. Let sit 10 minutes.

2. To dissolved yeast, add 1 cup warm milk and 1 cup flour. Beat with a whisk until smooth. Let rise in a warm place until bubbles appear, about 1 hour.

3. Beat yolks, then add sugar and beat until lemony in color. Add salt and rind. Add half the butter, the second cup of milk and 3 cups of flour. Beat thoroughly, adding yeast mixture and egg whites.

4. Add remaining flour to make a soft dough. Knead until smooth, about 10-15 minutes, adding in remaining butter and raisins. Let rise in a warm place until double. Punch down and let rise again.

5. Grease three 2-pound coffee tins and sprinkle lightly with fine breadcrumbs. Shape dough into smooth round balls and place in tin (should be ⅓ full). Let rise in a warm place until dough reaches the top of the tin.

6. Brush top carefully with beaten egg and a bit of milk or water. Bake at 350°F for 15 minutes, then 300°F for another hour. When done, let stand in cans 4-5 minutes, then carefully remove and place on a soft surface until completely cooled and firm.

7. To decorate Babka, mix together ½ cups icing sugar with ½ teaspoon lemon juice and enough warm water for a spreading consistency. Spread over top of the Babka and sprinkle with baker's confetti.

Makes 3 loaves.

Knysh

The kolach, or braided Christmas bread, is the traditional centerpiece for Sviat Vechir, or Christmas Eve. Knysh is bread with a filling, and in certain regions of Ukraine it constitutes another (albeit less known) type of Christmas bread. The knysh is specifically a reminder of deceased members of the family who are remembered at this meal.

Dough:
- **1 tbsp active dry yeast, regular or rapid**
- **1 cup warm water**
- **1 tbsp sugar**
- **2 tsp salt**
- **¼ cup oil**
- **3 cups flour or more, divided**

Filling:
- **2 large onions, finely sliced**
- **¼ cup oil**
- **Salt and freshly ground pepper**

1. Dissolve yeast and sugar in warm water. Stir in salt, oil and 2 cups of flour, mixing until smooth.

2. Blend in enough flour (1 to 1½ cups) to make a smooth dough. Knead for five minutes on a lightly floured surface and turn once. Cover with plastic wrap and let rise in a warm place until doubled.

3. Sauté onions in the oil on medium heat until tender and cooked through. Cool. Season to taste with salt and freshly ground pepper.

4. When dough has doubled, punch down and roll out onto a lightly floured surface into a 1-inch thick rectangle. Spread onion on dough and roll up like a jelly roll. Form into a circle on a greased baking sheet.

5. Slice loaf every inch (but not quite through to the center), twist slightly and fan out to make a beautifully shaped loaf. Let rise until doubled. Brush top with oil and bake at 350°F for about 50 minutes or until golden. Bread should sound hollow when tapped.

Makes 1 loaf.

Casseroles, Dumplings, & Side Dishes

Baked Millet Kasha

Millet is an ancient grain that until recently has been familiar to most North Americans primarily as a major component of bird seed. Fortunately, this small, round yellow grain is beginning to enjoy a renaissance with health-conscious humans. In addition to its significant health benefits, millet is delicately delicious and as easy to cook as rice. This millet kasha can be served with milk as breakfast cereal as well as with meat and gravy.

- **1 cup millet**
- **2 cups boiling water**
- **2½ cups boiling milk**
- **¼ cup butter**
- **1 tsp salt**
- **½ tsp sugar**

1. Rinse millet in a sieve under the tap until the water runs clear.

2. Put into a large saucepan. Pour about 2 cups of boiling water over it. Drain well.

3. Add boiling milk and remaining ingredients to the millet and bring to a brisk boil.

4. Stir a few times, then boil gently about 5 minutes, stirring constantly to prevent scorching and boiling over.

5. Pour the mixture into a casserole, roaster, or baking dish. Cover tightly with lid or foil.

6. Bake at 350°F for 45 minutes.

Serves 6.

Tip: For extra richness and a more traditional taste, substitute cream for some or all of the milk.

Buckwheat Kasha

Kasha is a term commonly applied to buckwheat, but it actually refers to any grain cooked like porridge. Buckwheat is to the Ukrainian what oatmeal is to the Scot! This simple buckwheat kasha recipe can be used by itself as a breakfast cereal, a side dish or an accompaniment to a clear broth.

- **1½ cups roasted buckwheat groats**
- **2 tbsp butter**
- **3 cups boiling water**
- **1 tsp salt**

1. Pour boiling water and salt over buckwheat.

2. Reduce heat, cover and simmer for 15 minutes.

3. Add butter, stir, then simmer another 15 minutes or so. Kasha is ready when fluffy and liquid is absorbed.

Serves 6.

Buckwheat Supper Casserole

This easy buckwheat casserole makes a simple but hearty meal that is a tasty treat for busy days. It's soul food! You can use ham, bacon or any double smoked sausage in this recipe. Also if you have any cooked mushrooms or other vegetables, throw them in!

- **1 cup toasted buckwheat groats**
- **½ cup diced onion**
- **2-3 tbsp butter**
- **1 lb Ukrainian garlic sausage**
- **3 cups water or soup stock**
- **Salt and pepper to taste**

1. Fry onion in butter until limp.

2. Add the sausage and fry a few minutes until browned.

3. Place onion, sausage and buckwheat groats in a casserole dish. Add water or soup stock, and salt and pepper to taste.

4. Bake for 1 hour at 350°F.

Serves 6-8.

Cabbage Rolls (Holubtsi)

Arguably the best-known Ukrainian dish is cabbage rolls — holubtsi in Ukrainian. This word means "little pigeons" in Ukrainian.

Cabbage rolls are very versatile and adaptable. In the summer time, beet, lettuce, or spinach leaves may take the place of cabbage leaves. The most popular filling today is rice, although originally grains native to the area, such as buckwheat and barley, were also used.

Cabbage rolls take a bit of time to make but the results are delicious and elegant. Serve with bacon bits and sour cream or other sauce.

To serve 10 people you will need about 3 lbs of softened cabbage leaves. To prepare them, first remove the core from a head of cabbage and place the cabbage in a large pot. Cover with water, add salt, and bring to a boil. Cook until the leaves start to separate.

Gently peel off the leaves with tongs, careful not to rip them, and place on a platter to cool. Cut the larger leaves in half and set aside any that are unusable. Trim the tough centre veins. Do not discard the trimmings! Save to put on the bottom of the roaster and/or on top of the layers before baking to prevent scorching.

Holubtsi may be cooked with or without a liquid, depending on the nature of the filling. A ready cooked filling requires little or no liquid. When a liquid is used, it may be one or a combination of several of the following: water, soup stock, tomato juice, tomato sauce (like Passata), meat drippings, sour cream. Some cooks like to use canned tomato soup, alone or in combination with sour cream, tomato juice, soup stock or water.

To make the cabbage rolls, place a tablespoon of filling on a cabbage leaf. Fold sides over filling and roll from bottom to top. Place rolls in layers in a casserole dish or roaster.

Drizzle holubtsi with 3-4 tablespoons of oil or dot with butter. Cover and bake at 350°F for 2 hours or more, until cabbage is very tender.

Rice Filling for Cabbage Rolls

Short grain rice is best for cabbage rolls. It holds together better than long grain, making it less likely the cabbage rolls will fall apart. Medium grain or sushi rice will work if you can't find short grain. Make sure to parboil the rice, rather than fully cook it, to keep the filling from getting mushy in baking.

- **2 cups short grain rice**
- **4 cups water**
- **2 tsp salt**
- **1 onion finely chopped**
- **½ cup butter, oil or bacon fat**
- **½ cup chopped crisp bacon, ground pork or ground beef**
- **Salt & freshly ground pepper**

1. Combine rice, water, and salt and bring to a boil. Cover and steam on low heat for 10 minutes.

2. Fry onion in butter or oil until golden.

3. Add to rice along with the bacon and/or meat of your choice. Mix well.

4. Season with salt and pepper to taste. Cool before using.

Buckwheat Filling for Cabbage Rolls

Roasted buckwheat, imported from Ukraine, is now available in most supermarkets and European delicatessens. If desired, you can add bacon, mushrooms, or other vegetables to this filling. However, tomato does not, in my opinion, enhance the taste of buckwheat. So for best results, don't add tomato juice, sauce or soup when baking these cabbage rolls.

- **2 cups roasted buckwheat groats**

- **4 cups water**

- **2 tsp salt**

- **1 large onion, finely chopped**

- **5 tbsp vegetable or olive oil, or butter**

- **Salt and freshly ground pepper**

1. Bring water and salt to a boil. Add the buckwheat and return to a boil. Cover and simmer 20 minutes. Cool.

2. Sauté onion in oil over medium heat until tender. Add to buckwheat. Season with salt and pepper to taste. Cool before using.

Tip: If you have only raw groats on hand, mix them with a beaten egg and brown them in a frying pan with a bit of butter, stirring frequently until slightly browned and crumbly. You can omit the egg if you prefer.

Potato Filling for Cabbage Rolls

While fillings for cabbage rolls are most commonly of rice and buckwheat, occasionally you may encounter something more unusual.

In the grape growing regions of Ukraine, this potato filling is often rolled in grape leaves. This practice, however, is strictly regional and not generally known to many Ukrainian cooks.

A few years back, while holidaying in Lviv, I was pleasantly surprised to be served cabbage rolls with potato filling. Different, and delicious!

- **4 large raw potatoes, finely grated and drained well**
- **1 small onion, finely chopped**
- **1 ½ cups thick sour cream**
- **½ cup roasted buckwheat groats**
- **Salt & freshly ground pepper**

1. Sauté the onion in butter until tender. Combine with the grated raw potatoes along with ½ cup sour cream.

2. Pour boiling water over the buckwheat groats and drain over a sieve. Repeat.

3. Add well-drained groats to the potato mixture. Season to taste. Cool before using.

4. Dilute remaining sour cream with a bit of water or stock, enough to make it pour easily over potato-filled cabbage rolls before baking.

Cabbage Roll Casserole with Ground Beef

Here's a perfect recipe for busy cooks who don't have the time to core, steam, and roll cabbage leaves for "proper" holubtsi, yet love the taste of this ubiquitous Ukrainian dish.

- **2 lbs lean ground beef**
- **3 tbsp oil**
- **1 large onion, finely chopped**
- **1 tbsp salt**
- **½ tsp freshly ground black pepper**
- **6 tbsp raw long grain rice**
- **2 cans tomato soup (10 oz)**
- **2 cans water**
- **1 tsp sugar**
- **6 cups shredded cabbage**

1. Sauté the ground beef in oil for a few minutes, then add onion, salt, pepper, rice.

2. Mix and continue frying for another 3-4 minutes.

3. Add soup, water and sugar.

4. Put half the shredded cabbage into a greased casserole dish, roaster, or baking dish.

5. Pour the meat mixture evenly over the cabbage. Top with remaining cabbage. To keep layers separate, do not stir.

6. Bake, covered, at 350°F for 1½ hours, or until cabbage is tender.

Serves 8.

Cabbage Roll Casserole with Bacon

For added tang, replace the cabbage (or a portion of it) with drained sauerkraut. Other fillings for cabbage rolls can also be used in this recipe, including buckwheat, cornmeal, millet, or potato filling.

- **5 strips bacon, diced**
- **1 large onion, finely chopped**
- **2 cups rice**
- **2 cups boiling water**
- **1 medium cabbage, chopped coarsely**
- **1 can tomato soup (14 oz)**
- **1 soup can of water**
- **Salt & freshly ground black pepper**

1. Fry bacon with onion, until onion is tender. Add cabbage and cook to wilt.
2. Cook rice in boiling water for 5 minutes.
3. Add bacon and cabbage mixture to rice along with tomato soup, a soup can of water, and seasoning.
4. Mix all ingredients together and pour into a deep 9x13 inch baking dish.
5. Cover and bake for 1½ hours at 350°F or until cabbage is tender.
6. Serve hot with a dollop of sour cream, if desired.

Serves 6.

Tip: Use your rice cooker to quickly and easily prepare millet, buckwheat, and other similar grains.

Vegetarian Cabbage Roll Casserole

This meatless variation of lazy cabbage rolls is incredibly tasty and is very easy to make. The dill lends flavour to the rice but no added calories or fat. This dish is excellent as a side dish or a light vegetarian lunch. Pawlina told me that it has become one of her favorites.

- **2 cups rice, short grain**
- **4 cups boiling water**
- **2 tsp salt**
- **¼ cup fresh dill, chopped**
- **⅓ cup butter**
- **1 large onion, chopped finely**
- **6-8 cups cabbage, shredded**
- **1 cup tomato juice**
- **Salt and freshly ground pepper**

Topping:
- **1 cup thick sour cream**
- **1 cup tomato juice**
- **1 tsp sugar**

1. Butter a deep 9x9 inch baking pan.
2. Wash rice until water runs clear. Add to boiling water with salt.
3. Bring to a boil, stir and cook one minute. Lower heat to simmer, cover and cook 30 minutes or until done. Cool. Mix in and add chopped dill.
4. Sauté onion in butter until soft. Add the cabbage and cook to wilt.
5. Mix in 1 cup tomato juice. Season with salt to taste and generously with pepper.
6. Layer bottom of baking dish with half the cabbage. Add the rice and top with the rest of the cabbage.
7. Top with a mixture of sour cream, tomato juice and sugar.
8. Cover and bake for 1½ hours at 350°F or until cabbage is tender.

Serves 4.

Cabbage with Egg Noodles

This recipe gets us back to our roots – wonderfully easy to prepare, delicious, and nutritious.

- **2 cups shredded cabbage**
- **1 small onion, finely chopped**
- **¼ cup olive oil or butter**
- **1 tsp salt**
- **½ tsp black pepper, or more to taste**
- **4 cups cooked egg noodles (wide)**
- **Bread crumbs browned in butter**

1. Sauté cabbage and onion in oil or butter until very soft.
2. Add salt and pepper. (I like to go heavy on pepper in this recipe.)
3. Cook egg noodles, drain, then toss into hot cabbage.
4. Sprinkle with some bread crumbs browned in a little butter.

Serves 6-8.

Tip: For a zesty change, add 1 cup chopped sauerkraut to the sweet cabbage.

Kulesha

Corn is a common and favoured grain in Ukraine, and is a particular favourite of the Hutsuls, who live in the Carpathian mountains. This traditional cornmeal pudding is a staple for Hutsuls, and was also very popular among early Ukrainian immigrants to Canada. You'll rarely find kulesha in restaurants or even at banquets anymore, but is very easy to make. Those unfamiliar with Ukrainian cookery will find it somewhat similar to the Italian polenta.

- **1 cup cornmeal**
- **3 cups cream**
- **1 tsp salt**

1. Heat cornmeal in a heavy frying pan, over low heat. Stir constantly until very hot. Be careful not to scorch it.

2. Boil cream with salt and gradually add the cornmeal. Stir in until smooth and free of lumps.

3. Cook until fairly thick.

4. Spoon into a well buttered 9x9" baking dish.

5. Cover and bake at 350° for 30 minutes. Serve hot, with sour cream and cottage cheese, fried onions, or meat and gravy.

Serves 6.

Tip: To prevent and protect from splashback while cooking cornmeal, wear oven mitts and stir with a kulishyr or a long-handed wooden spoon.

Cornmeal Beet Leaf Rolls

Serve these savoury, flavourful rolls with sour cream, mushroom sauce, or onions fried in butter.

- **4-5 dozen large beet leaves**
- **4 cups water**
- **1½ tsp salt, or to taste**
- **1 cup cornmeal**
- **5 tbsp oil**
- **1 medium onion, finely chopped**
- **3 cloves garlic, minced**
- **Freshly ground black pepper**

1. Add salt to water and bring to a boil over medium high heat.

2. Slowly add cornmeal, stirring constantly. Lower heat and cook 5 minutes. Continue stirring constantly and then set aside.

3. Sauté onion in oil until slightly golden. Remove from heat, add garlic to onions, mixing to blend.

4. Add onion mixture to cornmeal. Cool.

5. Wash beet leaves, spread on a cookie sheet. Put in a 200°F oven to slightly wilt, about 5 minutes.

6. Take a leaf in the palm of your hand, place a large spoonful of filling in the centre, and roll up like cabbage rolls.

7. Layer in a very well oiled medium roaster. Add water to about half full. Drizzle with oil.

8. Cover and bake at 350°F for about 45 minutes, or until leaves are tender.

Makes about 4 dozen rolls.

Tip: The cornmeal filling is also delicious in cabbage rolls.

Savoury Bukovynian Nachynka

My mom was always in demand to make this wonderful cornmeal dish for Ukrainian weddings. I remember with great fondness those weddings – how beautiful the live music was and how I used to swirl around the dance floor with my father, standing on his shoes.

When I visited Ukraine recently, I noticed that in Bukovyna (where my mother's side of the family is from) nearly everyone grows corn. So it's no wonder nachynka is a traditional favourite there.

- **1 small onion**
- **½ cup butter**
- **1 cup cornmeal**
- **1 tsp salt**
- **3 tbsp sugar**
- **¼ tsp freshly ground pepper**
- **3½ cups milk**
- **½ cup cream**
- **3 large eggs, well-beaten**
- **3 tbsp chicken drippings (optional)**

1. Fry onion in butter until very tender. (This will take about 15 minutes and is very important to make good nachynka.)

2. Add cornmeal, salt, sugar and pepper to onions. Mix thoroughly so the cornmeal will be well-coated with butter.

3. Scald milk and add gradually, stirring until mixture is smooth. If you have chicken drippings on hand, this can make a delicious difference!

4. Cook until thickened, stirring constantly. Remove from the stove, blend in cream, then fold in the beaten eggs.

5. Spoon into a 2-quart buttered casserole dish and bake, uncovered, at 350° for 1 hour. It should have a crisp brown crust on the top and sides.

Serves 6-8.

Malay (Hutsulian Cornbread)

Malay is a traditional dish enjoyed by the Hutsul people in the Carpathian Mountains of Ukraine, where corn is a staple. It pairs well with stews, soups, or even just on its own with a slice of ham or feta cheese.

When I was growing up, we used to fry slices of cornbread in butter and enjoy them with Mom's homemade strawberry jam – absolutely delicious!

The recipe for malay varies across different localities, but corn remains the central ingredient. If you're a fan of cornmeal, you'll enjoy this modernized version of the native Hutsul cornbread recipe.

- **1 cup flour**
- **½ tsp baking soda**
- **1 1/2 tsp baking powder**
- **1/2 tsp salt**
- **1/3 cup sugar**
- **1 cup cornmeal**
- **2 eggs, slightly beaten**
- **1 cup sour milk or buttermilk**
- **1/4 cup melted butter**

1. Blend the flour with the cornmeal, baking soda, baking powder, salt and sugar.

2. Mix in the beaten eggs, sour cream or buttermilk, and melted butter. Don't over mix.

3. Pour into a buttered 8 by 10 inch pan, and bake at 400°F for 30 minutes.

4. These also make super cupcakes. Just use buttered muffin tins and bake for 25 minutes.

Serves 6-8.

Cottage Cheese Patties

Although Ukraine is not especially well-known for its cheese, it has long been a part of Ukrainian cuisine. Scythians, the ancient forebears of modern-day Ukrainians, produced and exported cheese. More recently, John E. Herbst, while United States Ambassador to Ukraine, was quoted in the magazine *Welcome to Ukraine* as being pleasantly surprised at the quality of Ukrainian cheese, which he considered the finest in the world. These savoury cottage cheese patties, known as syrnychky in Ukrainian, are best served hot with sour cream.

- **2 cups dry cottage cheese**
- **2 large eggs**
- **½ cup flour (about)**
- **3 tbsp butter**
- **½ tsp caraway seeds (optional)**
- **1 tsp salt**
- **Oil for frying**

1. Push cottage cheese through a sieve.

2. Beat eggs, salt, caraway seeds and about 6 tablespoons flour (use just enough to make firm enough to shape into patties).

3. Using wet hands, make 16 small patties and dip them in remaining flour sprinkled on a flat surface.

4. Fry 5-6 patties at a time, in 2 tablespoons hot (but not browned) butter. Add more butter as needed.

5. Brown on both sides, and remove patties to warmed platter.

Serves 4.

Country Potato Pancakes

This old-country recipe takes a bit of effort to prepare, but the flavour of these delicious savoury pancakes, called kartoplyanyky in Ukrainian, makes every minute worthwhile.

- **4 large raw russet potatoes, grated coarsely**
- **1 large egg, slightly beaten**
- **1 small onion, finely grated**
- **½ cup flour**
- **2 tsp salt**
- **Freshly ground pepper**

1. Mix all ingredients well.

2. Pour about ¼ cup batter per pancake into a heavy, well-greased hot skillet.

3. Fry pancakes on medium heat until each side is well browned.

4. Serve hot with sour cream.

Serves 4-5.

Tip: Use large, mature russets for best results.

Noodle Ring

This noodle ring is an elegant way to dress up plain noodles (called lokshyna in Ukrainian), and makes a dramatic impact when the centre is filled with chicken or fish, or creamed vegetables like mushrooms, peas or carrots. Superb with fish baked in sour cream. If you want to really wow your guests, use your own home-made egg noodles.

- **4 cups cooked egg noodles**
- **6 tbsp butter, melted**
- **1 cup hard cheese, grated**
- **6 large eggs, separated**
- **1 tsp salt**
- **1 cup cream (half and half)**

1. Combine noodles with butter and cheese.

2. Beat egg whites with salt until stiff and set aside.

3. Beat yolks and mix in the cream. Add to the noodles.

4. Fold in beaten egg whites.

5. Generously butter a ring mold and spoon in the mixture. Set the mold into a pan of hot water.

6. Bake at 350°F for 40 minutes or until mixture is set.

7. Unmold (while still hot) by placing a large serving platter over the mold and then inverting. Fill the centre with desired creamed vegetables, meat or fish.

Serves 4-6.

Tip: If you don't have a ring mold you can use a pie or cake tin.

Halushky (Dumplings)

Halushky are Ukrainian dumplings made of batter or a thick dough mixture, with various ingredients added for tenderness, texture, flavor, and nutritional value. The best halushky are light rather than heavy. They are superb served hot with meat and vegetables, as a tasty alternative to plain potatoes or rice. Try them with beef stew, or even on their own with mushroom gravy or sour cream and cottage cheese.

- **2 cups mashed potatoes**
- **1 large egg, slightly beaten**
- **¾ cup flour**
- **¼ cup fine bread crumbs**
- **Salt & freshly ground pepper**
- **Melted butter**

1. Mix together all ingredients thoroughly.

2. On a floured board, shape rolls to ½" thick and 2" in length.

3. Cook in rapidly boiling water for about 5-6 minutes. The dumplings will float to the top when they are ready.

4. Remove dumplings with a slotted spoon.

5. Place in a bowl and toss generously with melted butter.

6. Serve smothered with caramelized onion and sour cream.

Serves 2-4.

Drop Dumplings (Halushky)

A plate full of these lovely dumplings slathered with onions fried in butter and topped with sour cream makes a meal for me! But normally they are served as a delightful accompaniment to meat or poultry with rich, homestyle gravy. These drop dumplings are easier to make than filled dumplings. And quicker—you can make them in minutes!

- **¾ cup flour**
- **¾ cup cream of wheat**
- **2 tsp baking powder**
- **1 tsp salt**
- **½ cup cold butter**
- **2 eggs, slightly beaten**
- **¼ cup milk or buttermilk**
- **6 to 8 cups of salted water**

1. Mix, flour and cream of wheat, baking powder and salt.

2. Add the butter to the flour mixture and crumble to form a coarse meal.

3. Add the eggs and milk, stirring the batter until smooth.

4. In a large pot, bring 6-8 cups of salted water to a boil, then lower heat to a simmer.

5. Drop the batter with a tablespoon that has been dipped in the simmering salted water each time. Do not overcrowd.

6. Cover and simmer for 8 minutes. They will float to the top when they are done.

7. Remove with a slotted spoon into a buttered baking dish and keep warm in a slow oven, about 200°F, until all the dumplings are done.

Makes about 14 dumplings.

Perogies (Varenyky)

The origins of this stuffed dumpling are believed to be circa 500 BC. The Scythians and Circassians enjoyed them, as did the Khazars. The expertise of making the dough was thought to be brought from China by caravan traders passing across southern Ukraine on their way to what is now Istanbul, Turkey. In Ukraine, restaurants serve a wide and plentiful variety of these stuffed dumplings, which are known as varenyky (meaning, literally, "boiled things"). In Canada, they are more commonly known as perogies and have become a supermarket staple like frozen pizza. If you have only ever tasted supermarket perogies, try making them yourself. You'll be glad you did!

- **2½ cups flour**
- **1 tsp salt**
- **¾ cup water, warm**
- **2 tbsp oil**
- **1 large egg, beaten**

1. Mix liquids and add to flour and salt.

2. Knead dough on a lightly-floured surface until dough is smooth and elastic, about 4-5 minutes, adding flour as needed. Rest, covered, at room temperature ½ hour.

3. Roll out dough ⅛" thick or to desired thickness. Cut into 3-inch circles or squares.

4. Place a tablespoon of filling in the centre. Fold edges to make a half-moon or triangle. Pinch edges well to keep filling from leaking.

5. Place perogies on a tray lined with lightly floured towels without touching. Cover until ready to cook.

6. Drop into gently boiling water. Stir with a wooden spoon and cook 6-8 minutes, or until they rise to the top. Lift out with a slotted spoon. Toss with oil or melted butter.

7. Serve warm with fried onion and sour cream.

Makes about 5 dozen.

Potato Cheddar Filling for Perogies

Ukrainians who emigrated to Canada and the U.S. quickly developed an affinity for cheddar cheese, which was brought to North America by English immigrants. It didn't take long for Ukrainians to discover that cheddar made a very tasty addition to potato filling for perogies. True to their generous nature, Ukrainian immigrants (and their descendants) shared this delicious discovery with their fellow Canadians, and the potato-cheddar perogy has now become a Canadian classic.

- **8 large russet potatoes**

- **2 cups shredded cheddar cheese**

- **Salt and freshly ground pepper**

1. Peel and cube potatoes.

2. Boil in salted water until soft.

3. Drain, reserving liquid for perogy dough, potato bread, or homemade soup or gravy.

4. Add cheese to potatoes immediately. Mash well while still hot, until cheese is melted.

5. Season with salt and pepper to taste.

6. Cool before using.

Makes 8-10 cups filling.

Tip: Don't forget to try the other delicious fillings on page 25!

Boiling Water Perogy Dough

Here's a recipe for dough that calls for hot water in the dough. A food processor saves time, but it can be made by hand as well using a wooden spoon to mix in the water.

Whatever dough recipe you use to make perogies, make sure that when you drop them in the water, it is simmering gently. Rapid boiling will cause them to burst. This dough (like most perogy dough) is freezer-friendly.

- **5 cups flour**
- **2 tsp salt**
- **½ cup oil**
- **2 cups boiling water**

1. Place flour, salt and oil in food processor bowl.

2. Through the spout pour boiling water and pulse to mix well.

3. Add a little more flour if the dough is too sticky, but only enough for it to remain very soft and easy to handle. It should come away from the sides of the bowl easily.

4. Roll out dough ⅛" thick (or thicker if preferred). Cut into 3-inch circles or squares and fill as desired.

5. Drop into gently boiling water. Stir with a wooden spoon and cook 6-8 minutes, or until they rise to the top. Lift out with a slotted spoon. Toss with oil or melted butter.

6. Serve perogies with sour cream, chopped onion fried in butter, or fried bacon bits.

Makes about 5 dozen.

"Diet" Perogies

I remember my mom making these for us. We used to call them shkirky, meaning "skins" in Ukrainian. The concept of a "diet" perogy is mine, and it comes from having no filling and using dry cottage cheese in the dough—which, unlike cheddar, is made from skim milk and therefore is lower in calories. Ok, it's a bit of a stretch. But for dieters who find life isn't worth living without perogies, this dish (especially if served with plain or Greek yoghurt) is a little less fattening than traditional perogies swimming in butter and sour cream!

- **2 cups dry cottage cheese**

- **1 tbsp melted butter**

- **3 large eggs, beaten**

- **1 tsp salt**

- **1¾ cup flour, or more**

1. Press cottage cheese through a sieve. Beat in butter, eggs and salt. Add enough flour to give the desired consistency for shaping.

2. Place dough on a well-floured board and shape into a long narrow roll. Flatten roll to ⅛" to ¼" thick. Make a slantwise criss-cross pattern with the back of a butter knife, about 2" wide.

3. Cut along ridges. If you like them smaller, cut the squares into triangles.

4. Drop in small batches into boiling salted water, stir very gently with a wooden spoon, and cook 6-8 minutes or until they are well-puffed. Remove to a colander to drain.

5. Place perogies in a warm dish and sprinkle with a small amount of olive oil or a pat of butter. Toss lightly to coat evenly. Keep warm until serving.

Makes about 2 dozen.

Ribbon Perogies

There are many time-saving modern adaptations for busy cooks whose families love perogies. No filling or pinching required with this quick and easy recipe.

- **3 cups mashed potatoes**
- **3-4 cups flour**
- **1 tbsp salt**
- **½ cup oil**
- **½ cup water**

1. In a large bowl blend the mashed potatoes, salt, and 3 cups of the flour thoroughly.

2. Make a well in the centre and add the liquids. Mix with a fork until smooth. Add a little more flour if dough is too sticky — but go slowly as adding too much will toughen the dough.

3. Knead on a floured board until dough is soft, adding flour as necessary.

4. Roll out to one-half inch thickness. Cut into strips one-half inch wide and 3 inches long.

5. Drop strips into salted boiling water (about 10 cups water with 2 tbsp salt). Cook uncovered until the "ribbons" float to the top, about 5-6 minutes.

6. Drain thoroughly in a colander.

7. Toss with your favourite sauce, or simply diced onion that has been sautéed in oil or butter.

Makes about 5 dozen.

Lazy Perogies

Here's another North American adaptation that requires no filling or pinching. It's even faster and easier if you use pre-cooked lasagne noodles.

- **9 lasagne noodles**
- **1 tsp salt**
- **2 cups dry cottage cheese**
- **1 large egg**
- **2 tsp onion salt**
- **1 cup sharp cheddar cheese, shredded**
- **2 cups mashed potatoes**
- **1 cup finely chopped onion**
- **¾ cup butter**
- **Salt & freshly ground black pepper**

1. Cook lasagne noodles with salt according to package directions.

2. Place 3 noodles in bottom of a 9x13 inch pan.

3. Combine cottage cheese, egg, onion salt and salt and pepper to taste.

4. Place over noodles. Cover with 3 more noodles.

5. Combine cheddar cheese with mashed potatoes and seasonings.

6. Place over noodles. Cover with 3 more noodles.

7. Sauté chopped onion in butter and pour over top noodle layer.

8. Cover and bake at 350°F for 30 minutes. Let stand 10 minutes before serving.

Serves 4-5.

Tip: For a traditional treat, cube and fry side pork (uncured bacon) to sprinkle over perogies. Ukrainians call these cracklings shkvarki. And make sure to save the fat – it's the purest kind of lard and perfect for making pies and biscuits.

Vushka ("Little Ear" Dumplings)

Tiny stuffed dumplings can be found in many different cuisines. Italians call similar pasta tortellini, and the Chinese call theirs wonton. Ukrainians call theirs vushka, or "little ear dumplings" because they look like little ears (vushka in Ukrainian). These mushroom and onion stuffed morsels are traditionally served in a clear broth and specifically with borshch on Christmas Eve. However, they make scrumptious appetizers any time of the year, especially served with bacon bits or butter-fried onion.

- **Perogy dough (see page 150)**
- **1 small onion, finely chopped**
- **1 lb fresh mushrooms, finely chopped**
- **3 tbsp bread crumbs**
- **1 tsp oil or melted butter**
- **Chopped fresh dill**
- **Salt & freshly ground pepper**

1. Sauté onion in oil until tender. Add mushrooms and sauté until tender. Season to taste with salt, pepper and dill. Add bread crumbs. Cool.

2. On a lightly floured surface, roll out dough ⅛ inch thick. Cut into 2 inch squares. Place a teaspoon of filling in center of each square. Fold into a triangle. Pinch edges tightly to seal. To make "ears," join two corners together in the shape of circle. Place vushka, uncovered, on trays lined with flour-dusted towels.

3. Drop 10-12 vushka into gently boiling salted water. Stir once with a wooden spoon.

4. When they float to the top, cook one more minute, then remove with a slotted spoon. Toss gently with oil.

5. Place 2-3 vushka in each soup plate and pour hot clear borsch or broth over them.

Makes about 5 dozen.

Buckwheat Varenyky with Sour Cherry Filling

This has to be one of the ultimate varenyky (aka perogy) recipes! Buckwheat flour is what gives these fruit-filled dumplings their delightful, unique flavour.

Dough:
- **1½ cups all purpose flour**
- **1 cup buckwheat flour**
- **1 tsp salt**
- **3 eggs, separated**
- **¾ cup milk**

Filling:
- **1 large jar (28 ounces) of sour cherries**
- **1/2 cup sugar, or to taste**

1. Sift both flours with salt into a medium mixing bowl.

2. Add the egg yolks and enough milk to form a stiff dough.

3. Knead dough on a lightly floured surface until very smooth. Roll into a ball and cover for about 30 minutes.

4. Mix cherries and sugar. Cook over medium heat for five or six minutes. Drain, but set aside the juice for serving. Cool cherries.

5. Divide dough in half. Roll out dough on a floured work surface to about an eighth of an inch thick. Cut in rounds with a 3 inch cookie cutter.

6. Beat egg whites until frothy and light. Brush a bit onto each round.

7. Place a spoonful of the filling on each round and bring sides together to form a half moon. Pinch the edges together to seal tightly.

8. Drop dumplings into a large pot of simmering salted water. Do not overcrowd and do not boil or they may burst. Simmer until they float to the surface, about 6 minutes.

9. Remove with a slotted spoon into a buttered casserole. Drizzle with butter and keep them warm in a 200°F oven. Serve with more melted butter, sour cream and the cherry syrup.

Makes 24-30 varenyky.

Mushroom Strudel

Making strudel is a snap with phyllo pastry! Nice served with a sweet or sour cream mushroom sauce, a fresh garden salad and crusty bread.

Filling:
- **1 lb lean pork sausage or ground pork**
- **3 cups mushrooms, finely chopped**
- **6 green onions, thinly sliced**
- **8 oz. cream cheese, diced**
- **1 tsp salt**
- **1 tsp freshly ground pepper**

Pastry:
- **18 sheets phyllo pastry, thawed**
- **½ cup olive oil or melted butter**
- **½ cup fine dry bread crumbs**

1. Cook meat over medium heat until it turns pink. Drain fat, add mushrooms and onions.

2. Continue cooking until meat is browned and vegetables are tender.

3. Drain off any liquid. Stir in cream cheese until blended. Add salt and pepper to taste.

4. Place a sheet of phyllo on a dry work surface. (Cover remaining sheets to avoid drying out.) Brush each sheet with oil or melted butter. Sprinkle with bread crumbs.

5. Repeat to make a stack of 6.

6. Place ⅓ filling in a row on the short side of the top sheet, 2 inches from the bottom edge and within 2 inches of outside edges. Fold ends over and roll up lengthwise.

7. Brush top with oil or butter. Score down 3-4 sheets with a very sharp knife, about 2 inches apart. Place on a parchment-lined baking tray. Repeat for other 2 strudels.

8. Bake in preheated oven at 375°F until golden, about 30 minutes. Let rest 10 minutes before serving. Cut into slices with a serrated knife.

Makes 3 strudels.

Pork Tenderloin & Mushroom Casserole

Ukrainians have a special fondness for mushrooms. In Ukraine, as in North America, there are many varieties of mushrooms to choose from. And fortunately, they are now available fresh year round in most supermarkets and green grocers. For this recipe cremini mushrooms (also called Italian or Roman brown) are recommended. Cremini mushrooms are cocoa brown and firmer, with a meatier flavor than the common white mushroom.

- **4 slices smoked bacon, chopped**
- **1½ cups sliced mushrooms**
- **1 large onion, chopped finely**
- **2 lbs pork tenderloin**
- **½ cup water**
- **½ cup thick sour cream**
- **Flour for coating**
- **Salt and freshly ground pepper**

1. In a skillet, sauté the bacon until crisp. Remove from pan and set aside.

2. Brown mushrooms and onions in the bacon fat. Remove and set aside with the bacon.

3. Cut the pork tenderloin into 1-inch thick slices.

4. Dip the slices of pork in flour seasoned with salt and pepper and fry in the remaining fat. If necessary, add some oil.

5. Arrange pork in a casserole, alternating with the bacon, onion and mushroom mixture. Season.

6. Combine the water and sour cream, season with some salt to taste and pour over the layers.

7. Cover and cook at 350° for about 35 minutes.

Serves 4.

Tip: Use full fat sour cream (14% butterfat) to keep sauce from being too watery.

Potato and Egg Casserole

This easy casserole makes a satisfying meatless lunch or supper, or a change from scalloped potatoes.

- **1 large onion, finely chopped**

- **3 tbsp butter**

- **4 large potatoes, cooked and sliced**

- **5 large eggs, hard-cooked and sliced**

- **1 cup sour cream**

- **¼ cup buttered bread crumbs**

- **Salt & freshly ground black pepper**

1. Cook onion in butter until very soft.

2. Arrange alternate layers of the potatoes, onion, and egg in a buttered casserole dish.

3. Season each layer well with salt & pepper.

4. Finish with a layer of potatoes, cover with sour cream, and top with buttered bread crumbs.

5. Bake, uncovered, at 350°F for 30 minutes.

Serves 4.

Country Potato Puff Casserole

The potato is a versatile vegetable that can be served plain or dressed up for elegance. Like good breads, it has a lovely flavour and hearty quality that make it welcome at all meals. It goes with a wide variety of seasonings and flavouring and can be cooked by any method. Whenever possible, cook potatoes with the skins on, as much of the food value is lost if peeled away. After cooking, the skins will slip off easily. This simple recipe is outstanding – puffy, egg-rich and very tasty!

- **5 cups boiled potatoes**
- **½ cup cream**
- **9 large eggs, lightly beaten**
- **1 tsp baking powder**
- **1 tbsp salt**
- **1 tbsp oil or melted butter**
- **Freshly ground black pepper**

1. Boil potatoes, drain and mash, blending in cream.

2. Add beaten eggs, salt and pepper to the mashed potatoes.

3. Add melted butter or oil and baking powder. Beat well.

4. Pour mixture into a well-greased 9x12 inch baking dish and bake for 20 minutes in a preheated 400°F oven.

5. Reduce heat to 350°F and bake another 20 minutes or until well-browned.

6. Serve hot with a dollop of sour cream, or a generous dose of melted butter.

Serves 8.

Egg Noodle and Spinach Casserole

Green vegetables like spinach should be cooked without a cover to permit the volatile acids to escape. This also helps preserve their green colour. For a delicious variation you can replace the spinach with shredded cabbage that has been sautéed with the onion.

- **4 cups cooked egg noodles**
- **1 cup grated cheese (your choice)**
- **½ tsp salt**
- **4 cups cooked spinach**
- **1 medium onion, finely chopped**
- **2 tbsp butter**
- **¼ cup buttered bread crumbs**
- **Salt & freshly ground pepper**

1. Combine the cooked noodles with the cheese and salt.
2. Squeeze the spinach dry, chop.
3. Fry the onion in the butter until very soft.
4. Add spinach and seasonings.
5. Butter a small baking dish and arrange the noodles and spinach in alternate layers.
6. Top with buttered bread crumbs.
7. Bake in a preheated oven at 350°F for 30 minutes.
8. Remove from oven, garnish with sliced hard-cooked eggs.

Serves 4.

Baked Sauerkraut with Sausage

Sauerkraut goes very well with pork, especially smoked pork. In this recipe, which combines sweet cabbage with sauerkraut, the amount of meat can be adjusted according to your personal taste.

- **2 lbs sliced Ukrainian sausage, or bacon**
- **1 can sauerkraut (28-oz)**
- **1 small cabbage, shredded**
- **1 small onion, chopped**
- **1 tsp salt**
- **¼ tsp sugar**
- **Freshly ground black pepper**

1. Drain sauerkraut, rinse if too salty, and chop.
2. Add cabbage, onion, salt, pepper, sugar and bacon or sausage.
3. Mix well.
4. Bake, covered, in an ungreased dish for one hour at 350°F.

Serves 6.

Tip: If you can't find Ukrainian sausage, Bavarian smokies or other smoked sausages work nicely in this recipe.

Meat & Seafood

Roast Duck

Ducks and geese are plentiful in Ukraine, bred not only for their delicious meat but also for their highly prized down and feathers.

Ancient Ukrainian custom dictates that a bride must have at least two large pillows and a feather bed cover called a peryna, which is filled with choice feathers and down of geese and ducks. If the family has a girl of marriageable age, they began preparation of these articles well in advance of the wedding.

Many people are intimidated at the thought of roasting duck, but this recipe makes it easy.

- **1 large duckling**
- **½ cup flour, seasoned with salt and pepper**
- **⅓ cup oil**
- **¼ cup water**

1. Wash, dry, and cut duckling into 4 pieces. Salt.

2. Dust each piece in seasoned flour and brown, skin side down, in hot oil.

3. Add ¼ cup water.

4. Cover and bake at 350°F until very tender and golden, about 1½ hours, or until leg joint moves freely.

Serves 2-4.

Chicken Kiev

To this day, there is no definitive history of this dish. One version is that it was invented in Russia in the early 20th century and later re-named after the Ukrainian capital, Kyiv (spelled Kiev in Soviet times). Another is that the dish was dubbed Chicken Kiev in New York to appeal to East European immigrants living there. Whatever its history, with a name and a flavour like it has, Ukrainians naturally adopted it as their own. For fewer calories but an equally rich taste, replace the butter filling with seasoned sliced mushrooms sautéed in butter. For an elegant variation, mix ½ cup Ukrainian brynzia, feta, Swiss, or other favourite cheese into the butter. For another variation, mix in 4 tablespoons chicken liver paté before chilling.

- **4 large chicken breasts, skinless, boneless**
- **1 cup butter**
- **2 large eggs, beaten**
- **1 tbsp water**
- **Salt and freshly ground pepper**
- **Seasoned flour**
- **Fine bread crumbs**

1. Place each breast between wax paper or plastic wrap and pound flat with a flat-surfaced mallet to about ¼ inch thickness. (Or ask your butcher to flatten them for you.)

2. Shape butter into 4 rolls, allowing 1 roll per cutlet. Chill until hard.

3. Sprinkle cutlets with salt and pepper and place one roll of butter on each cutlet. Wrap breasts around each piece of butter, creating 4 parcels. Secure with skewers if necessary.

4. Dust each cutlet with seasoned flour, dip into egg mixed with water, and roll in bread crumbs.

5. Fry in deep hot fat, 340° F for 5 minutes or until golden. Or brown quickly in hot butter, drain, and place in 400°F oven about 10 minutes.

6. Serve with mushroom sauce. Serves 4.

Tip: Make sure to use very fine bread crumbs for a crispy coating. (Use a flour sifter.)

168

Chicken Livers in Sour Cream

Chicken livers and sour cream are an unusual but intensely delicious flavour combination. This dish is a family favourite.

- **1 lb fresh chicken livers**
- **2 tbsp butter, or oil**
- **1 small onion, finely chopped**
- **1 tsp salt**
- **1 cup sour cream**

1. Wash livers and remove any membrane. Cut in half.

2. Sauté onion in butter or oil until soft and lightly browned.

3. Add the livers, sprinkle with salt and sauté about 8 minutes, depending on the size of the livers. (Be careful not to overcook — the livers should be soft, with slightly pink centres.)

4. Add sour cream and bring to a boil. Serve hot.

Serves 4.

Tip: Remember that chicken livers are the only livers that can be salted while cooking without toughening them.

Creamed Chicken

This recipe is a great make-ahead dish that lends itself to many variations. For example, use sour cream instead of sweet cream. Add sliced mushrooms or other vegetables, like carrots or parsnips.

I grew up on this scrumptious Ukrainian dish, made with fresh dill and sweet cream. Always use fresh dill if at all possible. It's much more flavourful than dried, and is available at most supermarkets year round.

- **3 lbs frying chicken, cut into 8 pieces**
- **½ cup flour**
- **½ tsp salt**
- **1 cup whipping cream**
- **2 tbsp fresh dill, finely chopped**
- **Freshly ground pepper**
- **Butter (enough for browning)**

1. Combine flour, salt and pepper and coat chicken pieces.

2. Brown in butter, then place in a casserole dish. Sprinkle with salt and pepper.

3. Combine dill with cream, and pour over chicken.

4. Cover and bake at 350°F for about 1 hour or until tender.

5. Serve with potato dumplings (halushky).

Serves 4.

Tip: Dill can be frozen for later use. Freezing keeps its fresh flavor. Just chop finely and store in the freezer in a plastic container.

Chicken in Dill Sauce

Dill is a much-loved herb in the Ukrainian kitchen. Its soft taste marries well with sweet or sour cream.

This recipe for chicken in dill sauce is a winner! And it is very old-world. For a variation, use sour cream instead of sweet cream, and add a cup of peas towards the end and cook another ten minutes.

- **1 frying chicken cut into serving pieces**
- **1/2 cup flour**
- **2 tsp salt**
- **½ tsp ground pepper**
- **4 tbsp oil or butter for frying**
- **1 cup water or chicken broth**
- **1 small onion, finely chopped**
- **1 clove garlic minced**
- **1 tbsp fresh dill, chopped**
- **1 cup whipping cream**
- **2 tbsp flour**

1. Mix ½ cup flour, salt and pepper. Coat chicken pieces with the flour mixture.

2. Brown the chicken slowly in oil or butter or a mix of both.

3. Add the onion and garlic to the chicken and sauté for two minutes.

4. Add water or broth and cook over low heat, covered for 40 minutes, stirring occasionally.

5. Blend 2 tbsp flour with the cream, mixing well to avoid lumps. Add dill and mix into the chicken.

6. Heat to cook the flour about five minutes, but do not boil.

7. Serve with rice, noodles or potatoes.

Serves 4.

Cutlets (Ukrainian Style)

Serve these delectable cutlets with mushroom gravy and a side dish of buckwheat, millet or cornmeal.

- **1 lb ground beef, lean**
- **1 lb ground pork**
- **4 oz anchovies, chopped**
- **½ cup milk**
- **1 large egg**
- **1 tbsp breadcrumbs**
- **1 tsp salt**
- **1 tsp freshly ground pepper**
- **1 small onion, finely chopped**
- **1 cup mashed potatoes**
- **½ cup flour**
- **¼ cup oil for frying**
- **2 cups stock, chicken or beef**
- **2 whole bay leaves**

1. In a large bowl, mix the meats with the chopped anchovies.

2. Add in the milk, egg, breadcrumbs, salt and pepper, chopped onion, potatoes and mix well.

3. Shape meat into 2 inch balls, roll in flour, and flatten into ovals.

4. In a large heavy skillet, brown cutlets in medium-hot oil, turning once.

5. Pour in stock. Add bay leaves.

6. Cover and simmer 15 minutes. Remove bay leaves before serving.

Serves 6-8.

Chicken with Mayonnaise

This buffet dish for chicken with mayonnaise is always a hit at parties. It's an attractive dish, easily prepared and never fails to delight.

- **4 lbs cooked chicken, skin and bones removed**

- **1 cup mayonnaise**

- **2 tsp prepared mustard**

- **3-4 tbsp sour cream**

- **1 tsp sugar**

- **1 tbsp lemon juice**

- **Paprika**

- **Tomato slices**

- **Cucumber slices**

1. Keep cooked chicken pieces large.

2. Combine the mayonnaise with the mustard, sugar, sour cream and lemon juice.

3. Arrange the chicken pieces on a platter and pour the mayonnaise sauce over them to cover each piece.

4. Sprinkle paprika on top and surround the chicken pieces with tomato and cucumber slices.

Serves 8-10.

Tip: Some varieties of cultured sour cream can curdle when heated, so you may want to thicken it with a bit of flour before adding it to this (or any) recipe.

Braised Short Ribs of Beef

Beef short ribs have a nice robust flavour, and fortunately they are a relatively inexpensive cut. The sour cream in this traditional recipe gives it a touch of elegance — and ultimate flavour.

- **2 lbs short ribs of beef**
- **1 clove garlic, crushed**
- **Seasoned flour**
- **2 tbsp fat for frying**
- **1 small onion, chopped**
- **½ cup hot water**
- **½ cup tomato juice**
- **Salt and freshly ground pepper**
- **1 large carrot, diced**
- **2 stalks celery, diced**
- **1 small red pepper, sliced**
- **3 tbsp sour cream**

1. Rub each piece of beef with the crushed garlic.

2. Dip in seasoned flour and brown in hot fat.

3. Add the onion, hot water, tomato juice, salt and pepper.

4. Cover and cook in a 350°F oven for 1½ hours, or until nearly tender.

5. Then add the vegetables and continue cooking for about ½ hour, or until the ribs and vegetables are done.

6. Season the sauce to taste.

7. Stir in sour cream. Serve with your favorite dumplings, potatoes or other side dish.

Serves 4.

Tip: Ask your butcher to cut the ribs into serving pieces.

Beef Patties with Horseradish Stuffing

These beef patties with horseradish stuffing take no more effort to make than plain meatballs and gravy. Start with your favourite meatloaf recipe, add the finishing touches below, and end up with a traditional and unique dish that will add an elegant touch to any meal or appetizer platter.

- **4 cups prepared meatloaf, raw**

Stuffing:
- **2 large egg yolks, hard-cooked, sieved**
- **⅓ cup horseradish, freshly grated**
- **2 tbsp melted butter, or oil**
- **2 tbsp soft bread crumbs**

Gravy:
- **2 tbsp flour**
- **½ cup soup stock or water**
- **½ cup thick sour cream**

1. Make patties out of meat loaf mixture.

2. Mix stuffing ingredients until well-blended. Place a heaping teaspoonful of stuffing on each patty, turn up the edges over the filling, and shape into balls or ovals.

3. Brown the meatballs in hot butter or oil. Place in a baking dish.

4. Make gravy by blending flour with the fat in the pan, and adding ½ cup soup stock or water.

5. Bring to a boil and add ½ cup sour cream.

6. Pour sauce over the meat. Cover and bake at 350°F for 30 minutes.

Serves 6.

Tip: Prepared horseradish can be used but you'll have the best results if you use freshly grated horseradish.

Stovetop Meatloaf with Carrots

Carrots add colour to this meatloaf as well as fibre and added nutrients. Sautéing them along with the onions brings out their sweet flavour, adding a more intense flavour. The sour cream, characteristic in Ukrainian meat cookery, blends with the meat extracts to add a rich tang. This recipe is equally delicious as a skillet dish or as a traditional baked meatloaf.

- **3 large carrots, diced**
- **1 large onion, thinly sliced**
- **2 lbs ground beef**
- **4 tbsp butter or olive oil**
- **2 tbsp flour**
- **4 tbsp water**
- **2 tbsp tomato paste**
- **1 cup sour cream**
- **Salt and freshly ground pepper**

1. Sauté carrots and onions in butter or oil in a heavy skillet over medium-low heat, until soft.

2. Add beef and cook until no longer pink.

3. Sprinkle with flour and mix thoroughly.

4. Add water, tomato paste, half the sour cream, and salt and pepper.

5. Continue cooking until done.

6. For a baked meatloaf, mix sautéd vegetables, meat, flour, water, tomato paste and half of the sour cream, and place meat mixture in a loafpan or casserole dish. Bake at 350°F for 45 minutes.

7. Top meatloaf with remaining sour cream before serving, or put the cream in a serving bowl and pass it around the table.

Serves 8.

Basic Meatloaf

Although meatloaf is often considered a budget dish or "comfort" food, when stuffed it becomes elegant enough to serve at dinner parties. This basic meatloaf lends itself to a variety of stuffings, but is delicious on its own.

- **¾ cup dried bread crumbs**
- **1 cup milk**
- **1 small onion, grated**
- **3 tbsp butter**
- **1 lb lean ground beef**
- **½ lb ground veal**
- **½ lb ground lean pork**
- **1 large egg, slightly beaten**
- **½ cup hot water**
- **1 tbsp flour**
- **½ cup sour cream or tomato juice**
- **Salt and freshly ground pepper**

1. Soak bread crumbs in the milk.

2. Sauté grated onion in the butter until soft.

3. Combine bread crumbs, onion, ground meat, and egg. Season with salt and pepper.

4. Lightly grease a loaf pan. Pat in mixture. Cover with greased aluminum foil and bake at 350°F for 1 hour. Halfway through baking, pour the hot water over it, cover and continue baking.

5. Remove foil for the last 15 minutes of baking.

6. When done, blend flour with the sour cream or tomato juice and pour over the meat. Continue to cook for another 10 to 15 minutes.

7. Remove meatloaf to a hot platter. Season sauce to taste, then strain and pour over sliced meat loaf.

Serves: 6-8.

Stuffed Meatloaf

This great buffet dish never fails to surprise and delight my guests. Stuff with whole hard-cooked eggs, whole long pickles, whole cooked carrots, cooked perogies, or 2 cups of your favourite bread stuffing, sauerkraut, or sautéed mushrooms. Or be adventurous and experiment to create your own special recipe.

- **3 lbs raw meatloaf mixture**

- **Stuffing of choice**

1. Divide meatloaf mixture into two. Place half of the mixture into a greased loaf pan or oven-proof dish.

2. Place filling down the centre (lengthwise). Lay eggs or vegetables end to end, or if using a stuffing mixture, place in a strip 1-2 inches wide.

3. Place remainder of meatloaf over the stuffing, covering from end to end and side to side. Pat down firmly.

4. Bake at 350°F for 35-40 minutes. Let rest for 10 minutes. Invert onto serving platter. Slice and serve, hot or cold.

Serves 6-8.

"Cool" Kovbasa

Kovbasa is traditional Ukrainian garlic sausage, and arguably the most ubiquitous (and beloved) of Ukrainian meats. This original recipe comes from a listener in Ukraine who shared it on the Nash Holos blog. According to him, contemporary Ukrainians serve this hearty dish with sauerkraut salad and a shot of ice cold vodka.

- **½ lb lean kovbasa, sliced ½ inch thick**

- **¼ lb bacon**

- **¼ lb fatback, diced, or ¼ cup olive oil**

- **5 large potatoes, baked, peeled and quartered**

- **1 large onion, sliced thinly in rings**

1. In a large skillet, over medium low heat, fry the onion with the diced fatback or olive oil, until the onions are soft and slightly caramelized.

2. Add in the sliced bacon and fry until crisp.

3. Then add in the slices of kovbasa and potato wedges, mixing to coat with onion and bacon and to heat through.

4. Sprinkle with salt to taste.

Serves 5-6.

Tip: Fatback is a type of pork fat that comes from the back of a pig. It is a hard fat that can be used in various ways to add flavor, moisture and juiciness to different dishes.

Baked Ham

Ham is central to Easter dinner for Ukrainians, as it is in many other European cultures. In the old country tradition, Ukrainian hams were dried and smoke cured, and required special soaking and cooking. Today's commercially cured hams are wetter and heavier, and despite the "ready-to-eat" label do require some additional preparation. This method is ideal for busy cooks preparing an elegant festive meal.

- **6-8 lb ready-to-serve ham**

Glaze:
- **¼ cup prepared mustard**
- **½ cup brown sugar**

Baking Liquid:
- **1½ cups apple cider**
- **2 whole cloves**
- **1 small bay leaf**
- **Freshly ground black pepper**

1. Skin the ham and score the fat in diamond shapes so the glaze will soak in and stick to the ham.

2. Mix the mustard and sugar and spread on the ham.

3. Place the ham and other ingredients in a large roaster

4. Bake at 350°F for 1 – 1½ hours, basting three times during the last half hour of baking.

5. Tent with foil and rest for 15 minutes before carving, if serving warm.

6. Serve hot or cold, thinly sliced with beet relish, mayonnaise with horseradish and/or mustard assortment.

7. For extra beauty and flavor, place a clove into each diamond of fat before baking.

Serves about 12.

Studenetz (Jellied Lean Pork)

Studenetz is jellied lean pork, made from pork hocks and/or pigs feet. It is also called hyshka by some Ukrainian Canadians descended from the earlier immigrant era, and kholodetz by contemporary Ukrainians. This traditional dish is a culinary delight and highly nutritious. It is high in protein and taste, but very low in fat. It takes a bit of time to prepare, but is well worth the effort. To save time, use a pressure cooker.

- **6 large pigs feet, or 3 pork hocks, or a combination**

- **2 tbsp salt**

- **1 large onion**

- **5 cloves garlic (or to taste)**

- **1 dried bay leaf**

- **1 tsp freshly ground black pepper**

1. Soak meat overnight in salted water, covered, in the refrigerator.

2. Drain and wash thoroughly. Place in a large pot, add salt. Cover with cold water and bring to a boil. Skim off foam as it rises to the top, then add remaining ingredients.

3. Simmer until meat comes off the bones easily. (This will take several hours.) When done, separate the meat from the bones. Discard bones and cube or shred the meat.

4. Place meat in a 9x13 inch glass baking dish. Stir, then strain the liquid through a sieve over the meat. If desired, crush more garlic and add to liquid. Stir slightly and chill thoroughly until gelled.

5. Before serving, scrape any fat off the top and serve in slices or squares.

Serves 4-8.

Tip: As a make-ahead, you can freeze studenetz in jars or containers. Later, you can thaw, reheat, and chill it until gelled again.

Roast Loin of Pork

There is nothing like the taste of a good pork roast. The rub of flour, salt, sugar and mustard, along with the sweet-sour apple sauce makes this roast very special. It is also very easy to make and a lovely company dish. It's tender and juicy with an attractive brown coating.

Bake some whole small to medium sized apples with the roast during the last half hour of cooking – they make a wonderful accompaniment!

- **4 lbs pork loin**

Rub:
- **2 tbsp flour**
- **2 tsp salt**
- **½ tsp sugar**
- **1 tsp prepared mustard**
- **¼ tsp pepper**

Glaze:
- **1 cup applesauce**
- **⅓ cup brown sugar**
- **2 tsp vinegar**

1. Mix the flour, salt, sugar, mustard, pepper, and rub this in to the loin.

2. Place the loin, fat side up, in a roaster. Roast uncovered in a 350°F oven until done, allowing 20-25 minutes to the pound. Thermometer will read 170°F for well-done, or 160°F for medium.

3. During the last half hour of cooking, brush the roast generously with a mixture of applesauce, brown sugar, and vinegar (to glaze it), and continue cooking.

Serves 6-8.

Roast Pork Tenderloin with Caraway

Caraway seeds in the kitchen are a delight, both in savoury dishes and desserts, and go particularly well with rye bread, beets, potatoes, fresh cabbage, sauerkraut, and pork. The rub makes this tenderloin pork roast with caraway seeds especially delicious.

I like to place pork slices in a ring on the platter, then make an inside ring of creamy mashed potatoes, and in the centre place a heaping pile of sauerkraut that's been fried in some oil, finely chopped sweet onion, a sprinkle of pepper and a teaspoon of sugar. It's gorgeous, delicious and easy!

- **3-4 lbs pork loin**
- **1 large onion, finely chopped**
- **1 tsp caraway seed**
- **1 cup water**

Rub:
- **3 tbsp flour**
- **1 tsp salt**
- **½ tsp sugar**
- **1 tbsp prepared mustard**

1. Rub the flour and mustard mixture into the loin.

2. Place the seasoned meat in a roaster and add onion, caraway seeds and water. Cover and roast at 350°F until done, allowing 20-25 minutes to the pound.

3. Remove the roast and let rest for 5 minutes. Slice and arrange on a warm platter.

4. Strain the pan drippings and pour over the meat.

Serves 6.

Sage Stuffed Spareribs

The greenish-gray, long leaves of sage have a savory, dry aroma and somewhat spicy flavor – a natural counterbalance for rich and fatty foods. This traditional recipe for stuffed spareribs calls for a flatbread stuffing, but you can substitute 4 cups of cubed dried bread or crushed soda crackers.

- **6-7 lb length of spareribs**

Flatbread for Stuffing:
- **3 large eggs, well beaten**
- **½ cup water**
- **2 cups flour**
- **1½ tsp baking powder**
- **1 tsp salt**

Stuffing:
- **1 small onion, finely chopped**
- **1 stalk celery , chopped**
- **¼ cup butter**
- **2½ cups hot water or chicken stock**
- **5 large eggs, beaten**
- **3 tbsp flat-leaf parsley, chopped**
- **1 tsp fresh sage, chopped**
- **1 tsp salt**
- **1 tsp freshly ground pepper**

1. Beat the eggs with water. Add in dry sifted ingredients and mix well. Knead until smooth.

2. Roll to 1 inch thick. Place on a greased cookie sheet and prick with a fork in several places.

3. Bake at 350°F for 45 minutes. Cool and cut into small cubes.

4. Sauté onion and celery in butter and add to hot liquid. Pour over bread cubes. Cover and steam a few minutes.

5. Combine all the other ingredients and add to the bread mixture. Mix gently.

6. Trim excess fat from spareribs and generously salt-and-pepper them on both sides.

7. Lay ribs down in a roasting pan and cover with stuffing. Roll like a jelly roll. Tie securely.

8. Add half a cup water. Cover. Bake at 350°F for 2 hours, or until ribs are browned.

Serves 6-8.

Tip: A rack of ribs all the same size will make rolling much easier.

Spareribs with Sauerkraut

Another great make-ahead! For a great one-dish meal, add quartered potatoes towards the last half hour of cooking, and make a roux with browned flour and oil and mix in to thicken and intensify the flavour.

- **4 cups sauerkraut**
- **3 lbs pork spareribs, cut in pieces**
- **2 tsp salt**
- **1 large onion, diced**
- **1 cup boiling water**
- **½ tsp caraway seeds (or more)**
- **2 whole bay leaves**
- **2 tsp sugar**
- **Salt & freshly ground pepper**

1. Rinse sauerkraut if too salty or tart.

2. Brown ribs under broiler or in a frying pan with some oil.

3. Combine ribs and sauerkraut with remaining ingredients in a roaster.

4. Cover and bake at 375°F for 1½ hours or until tender. Remove bay leaves before serving.

Serves 6.

Tip: Pork neck bones can be used instead of spareribs.

Stuffed Pork Tenderloin

Over-cooking makes tender cuts of meats tough and dry. Today it is safe to cook pork only until pink — just make sure the juices run clear.

- **2 pork tenderloins, about 2 lbs each**
- **Melted butter**

Basic Bread Stuffing:
- **4 cups bread crumbs**
- **⅓ cup hot water (or enough to moisten the crumbs)**
- **1 small onion, chopped finely**
- **⅓ cup butter**
- **1 tsp poultry seasoning**
- **1 tbsp flat-leaf parsley or Italian, chopped**
- **Salt and freshly ground pepper**

1. Butterfly tenderloins by splitting lengthwise without cutting them through completely. Open each loin and flatten out with your hand or the flat side of a mallet.

2. Brush with melted butter and sprinkle with salt and pepper.

3. To make the stuffing, pour enough hot water over the bread crumbs to moisten. Sauté onion in the butter and mix into bread crumbs along with the seasonings.

4. Spread the stuffing on one flattened tenderloin and cover with the other one. Tie the roll in two or three places with kitchen string.

5. Brush the roasting pan with fat, put the roll in it and brush with butter or oil.

6. Cook in a 350°F oven until tender, allowing 20-25 minutes per pound.

7. Rest the roll five minutes before slicing. Serve with the pan juices.

Serves 6.

Tip: A meat thermometer is the answer for perfection. It should read 170°F for well-done, or 160°F for medium.

Shashlyky (Shish Kebobs)

Shashlyky is a Caucasian dish which the Ukrainians adopted many centuries ago. It is essentially the Ukrainian version of shish kebob and a great favourite throughout Ukraine. Originally the meat was threaded on swords and roasted over an open fire. Of course today we have modern-day flat metal skewers which can be used either outside (which is best) or inside. If broiling, place skewers on a broiler rack close to the heat. Turn skewers several times, basting with oil, until meat is cooked to desired doneness. The skewers can be prepared ahead, covered and kept in the fridge for several hours until ready to cook.

- **½ lb lean salt pork or unsliced bacon**
- **½ lb fillet of beef**
- **½ lb fillet of veal**
- **½ lb fillet of pork**
- **½ lb fillet of lamb**
- **Oil for basting**
- **Salt and freshly ground black pepper**
- **Sweet paprika**

1. Cut meat into 2" cubes.

2. Thread on skewers loosely, alternating the different meats. Leave a slight space between pieces rather than cramming them together, so the meat sears properly.

3. Brush and baste with oil. Grill, turning 2-3 times, until desired doneness.

4. Garnish with green onions, lemon wedges and tomatoes.

5. Sprinkle with paprika, salt and pepper.

Serves 6-8.

Tip: Make sure to use the flat metal skewers for this dish. Round wooden skewers are fine for hors d'oeuvres but they don't hold heavier meats well, and can become a safety hazard if they break.

Marinated Lamb Shashlyky

Whenever we marinate meats, it will change the flavour to some degree. Marinating does make meat more tender, which is why tough cuts are sometimes used for marinated lamb shish kebobs. Marinating enhances the delicate flavours of lamb, regardless of cut.

For a deluxe version of shashlyk and a very beautiful presentation, add the following, alternating with cubes of meat: firm cherry tomatoes, zucchini chunks, medium mushrooms, red onion pieces, white onion pieces, red or yellow pepper slices, bacon slices (for wrapping around the tomatoes or onions).

- **3 lbs boneless lamb pieces (2-inch cubes)**

- **Oil for brushing**

- **Assorted vegetables, cubed (optional)**

Marinade:

- **½ cup vinegar**

- **½ cup dry red wine**

- **1 large onion, chopped finely**

- **3 cloves garlic, mashed**

- **12 black peppercorns**

- **1-2 whole bay leaves**

- **½ tsp salt**

1. Prepare the marinade and cube the meat.

2. Put the meat with the marinade in a glass bowl, cover and let stand for 2 hours or longer at room temperature.

3. Drain, pat dry and skewer the meat pieces and vegetables. Brush with oil.

4. Cook over the grill, turning and basting with oil until desired doneness is achieved.

Serves 8-10.

Veal Paprika

While paprika is most commonly known as a typical spice of Hungarian cooking, paprika is used as an ingredient in a broad variety of dishes throughout the world, including Ukraine. This dish is lovely served with steamed rice, mashed potatoes or buckwheat kasha.

- **2 lbs veal steak**
- **Flour seasoned with salt and pepper for coating**
- **3 tbsp butter**
- **1 large onion, finely chopped**
- **2 tsp sweet paprika**
- **1 cup chicken or vegetable stock, or water**
- **1 cup sour cream**
- **Salt and freshly ground pepper**

1. Cut the meat into 2 inch squares.
2. Coat pieces with seasoned flour and brown lightly in the hot butter.
3. Add onion and brown lightly.
4. Remove skillet from heat, add paprika and mix thoroughly.
5. Return pan back to the heat, pour in stock or water and season with salt and pepper.
6. Cover and simmer 30 minutes.
7. Add sour cream and continue simmering slowly for another 10-15 minutes, or until tender.

Serves 4-6.

Tip: Hot paprika is not recommended for veal, as it will overpower the delicate flavour of the meat.

Baked Stuffed Salmon

When I was a newlywed, my husband and I used to fish for sturgeon near Mission in the Fraser Valley. We were often very lucky, but also very naïve. I'll never forget cleaning the sturgeon in my Mom's backyard one day. Mom was on the porch watching, and questioning why we were throwing away the eggs, or roe. Of course, we knew it all and had no use for the caviar—which we discovered far too late was worth hundreds of dollars. If only we had listened to Mom! This recipe for baked stuff salmon can also be used with sturgeon (if you are lucky enough to catch one!) or any white fish.

- **3-5 lb whole salmon, butterflied**
- **Salt & freshly ground pepper**

Stuffing:
- **½ cup butter**
- **1 medium onion, finely chopped**
- **½ cup celery, finely chopped**
- **3 cups soft bread crumbs**
- **1 large egg, beaten**
- **2 tbsp flat-leaf parsely, finely chopped**
- **1 tsp salt, or to taste**
- **1 tsp freshly ground pepper, or to taste**
- **½ cup water, or more**

Basting:
- **¼ cup olive oil or melted butter**

1. Remove any pin bones with sterilized tweezers. Season cleaned fish generously with salt and pepper inside and out.

2. Sauté onion, celery and parsley in butter, until tender. Combine with remaining stuffing ingredients, and season.

3. Stuff fish cavity and fasten opening with skewers or tie lightly with string. Brush with some oil or melted butter.

4. Bake on well-greased foil or parchment-lined baking tray at 425°F allowing 10 minutes per inch of thickness of stuffed fish.

5. Baste 2-3 times with oil or melted butter.

6. Garnish with sprigs of fresh dill or parsley and lemon wedges. Serve with your favourite fish sauce or dill cream sauce.

Serves 8-10.

Fish Baked in Sour Cream

Since Ukraine borders on the Black Sea, and is criss-crossed by several rivers, fish and seafood have long been central to Ukrainian cuisine. The sour cream in this recipe creates a rich sauce, making it perfect to serve over fluffy steamed rice, creamy mashed potatoes, or boiled tender new potatoes.

- **3 lbs white fish fillets (cod, halibut, or snapper)**

- **1 small onion, finely chopped**

- **1 medium carrot, diced**

- **1 stalk celery, diced**

- **1½ cups sour cream (14% butterfat)**

- **Salt & freshly ground pepper**

1. Cut fish into serving pieces. Generously salt and pepper the fish and place in a baking pan. Let stand 5 minutes.

2. Arrange vegetables around the fish.

3. Beat the sour cream slightly to make it easy to pour, then pour it over the fish and vegetables.

4. Cover and bake at 450°F for 9-10 minutes per inch of thickness.

5. When done, remove fish and vegetables from the pan onto a platter or serving dish, and pour sauce over the fish.

Serves 6-8.

Whitefish in Wine

Recent archaeological finds indicate that a wine culture has existed on the territory of modern-day Ukraine since at least the 4th century B.C. Today, Ukraine's wine industry is flourishing, as Ukrainian wine is highly prized by neighbouring countries. I don't know how far back this recipe goes, but it's been one of my favourites as long as I can remember.

- **2 lbs white fish fillets**
- **2 tbsp butter**
- **⅔ cup white wine**
- **⅓ cup water**
- **2 tbsp flour**
- **2 tbsp butter, melted**
- **1 egg yolk, slightly beaten**
- **Juice of 1 lemon**
- **Salt and freshly ground pepper**

1. Cut fillets into serving pieces. Season generously with salt and pepper.

2. Place the butter, wine, water and lemon juice in a large pan.

3. Arrange fish in the pan and bring to a boil. Lower temperature. Cover and simmer for 15 minutes.

4. Remove fish to a platter and thicken sauce. Make a paste of the flour and melted butter. Add the paste into the wine stock gradually, stirring and cooking until sauce thickens.

5. Spoon a little sauce into the slightly beaten egg yolk and then mix back in with rest of sauce.

6. Season to taste.

7. Strain the sauce, if desired, and pour over fish.

Serves 4.

Potato-Crusted Seafood Pie

This dish can turn any meal into a special occasion, and is elegant enough that it is sometimes served at Ukrainian weddings. Most types of fish can be used. Every time you change the fish, you'll change the flavour accordingly, so this recipe lends itself to many different variations.

- **1 lb white fish fillets - halibut, snapper or cod**
- **2 cups homogenized milk**
- **Salt and freshly ground pepper**

Sauce:
- **1½ cups mushrooms, sliced**
- **½ cup butter, divided**
- **½ cup flour**
- **3 medium tomatoes, peeled & diced**
- **½ lb shrimp or prawns, peeled and deveined**
- **1 tbsp lemon juice**
- **2 tbsp thick sour cream**

Topping:
- **3 cups potatoes, mashed with a little milk and butter**
- **2 tbsp finely chopped dill**

1. Bake fish fillets in milk, with salt and pepper, at 350°F for about 15 minutes or until done.

2. Strain milk into a bowl. Set aside.

3. Flake fish and remove any bones with a pair of sterilized tweezers.

4. Sauté mushrooms in ¼ cup butter.

5. Melt remaining butter in a saucepan. Stir in flour and continue to cook over medium low heat for 3 minutes.

6. Slowly add milk and continue cooking over low heat, stirring constantly until thickened.

7. Add mushrooms, shrimp or prawns, tomatoes, sour cream and lemon juice to the sauce. Taste, and adjust seasonings.

8. Put fish in a casserole and top with sauce.

9. Cover with a layer of mashed potatoes and sprinkle with chopped dill.

10. Bake at 350°F for 20 minutes.

Serves 6.

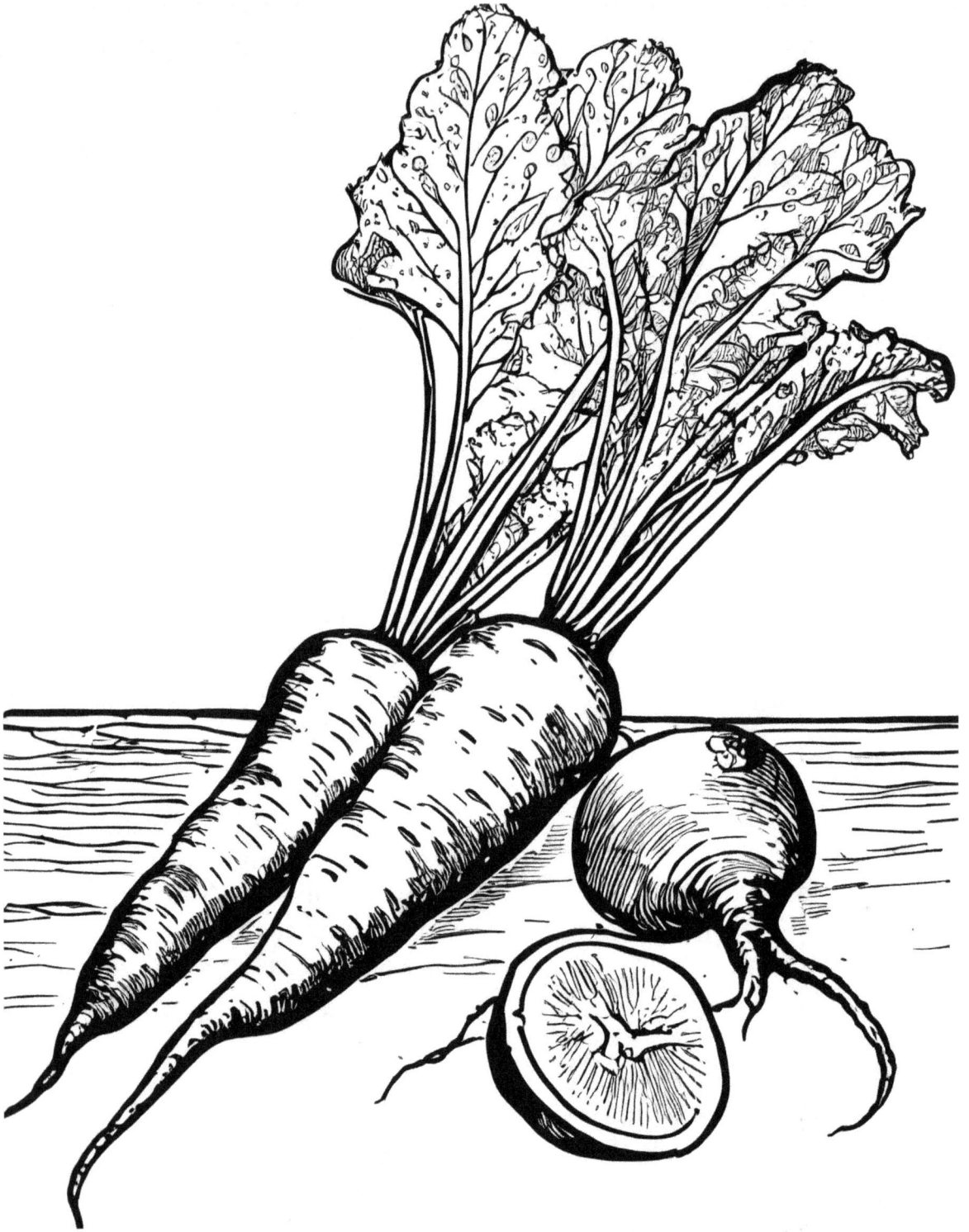

Vegetables

Asparagus with Honey & Sour Cream Dressing

This tangy sauce combines two ingredients favoured in Ukrainian cookery to create an elegant and unique accompaniment to any meat.

- **1 lb asparagus tips, cooked**
- **1 cup sour cream**
- **2 tbsp honey**
- **2 tbsp vinegar**
- **½ tsp dry mustard**
- **¼ tsp salt**

1. Combine sour cream, honey, vinegar, mustard and salt and gently heat. Do not boil.

2. Pour over asparagus tips.

3. This sauce is also delicious with cooked string beans, brussels sprouts, broccoli or diced beets.

Serves 4.

Tip: If you prefer not to use full-fat sour cream, be especially careful not to let the sauce boil, or it will separate. Full-fat sour cream will not do this.

Beets

Beets are highly nutritious with a robust, earthy flavour. Roasting or baking beets really brings out their sweetness, and makes cooking them particularly easy.

Baked grated beets are a delicious hot side dish that is very easy to prepare. A good rule of thumb is to allow about ½ cup beets per person. Stuffed beets are a unique and elegant cold side dish that is also a great make-ahead.

I find that baking beets in foil is the best method for cooking beets whole. It's the easiest, least messy and allows you to store the beets without handling them until you want to eat them. At that point, unwrap, peel and prepare them as you desire.

Baked Beets

1. Wash, peel, and grate raw beets coarsely.

2. Layer grated beets in a buttered baking dish.

3. Sprinkle each layer with salt, pepper, sugar and lemon juice or vinegar.

4. Dot with butter, cover dish with lid or foil.

5. Bake at 375°F for 1 hour or until fork tender.

Roasted Beets

1. Preheat oven to 400°F.

2. Place beets in the center of a large piece of aluminum foil, or wrap individually.

3. Fold up center and ends of foil to enclose beets.

4. Place foil packet(s) on a parchment-lined baking sheet and roast for about 1-1½ hours, or until tender when pierced with a thin bladed knife.

5. When cool, open the foil packet and slip off skins to prepare or serve. Or store for later use. Roasted beets will keep in an airtight container in the refrigerator for up to five days or in the freezer for up to three months.

Stuffed Beets with Vegetables

1. Roast number of beets required.

2. Cut a slice from the top of each beet and scoop out the pulp to make a shell. Save pulp for another use. Cut a thin slice from the bottom as well so they stand upright.

3. Prepare a filling of finely chopped celery, cucumbers and cabbage. Moisten with a salad dressing of your choice.

4. Fill each shell and top with a sieved or finely chopped hard-boiled egg yolk.

5. Garnish with parsley or dill sprigs if desired.

Stuffed Beets with Rice, Apples and Cheese

This traditional Ukrainian recipe for baked stuffed beets with rice, apples and cheese calls for farmers cheese.

This cheese is a form of cottage cheese from which much of the liquid has been pressed. Farmers cheese has a mild, slightly tangy flavor and is firm enough to slice, crumble or grate. It's usually available in most large supermarkets.

If you can't find farmers cheese, cow's feta or dry cottage cheese are good substitutes.

- **5 large beets, cooked**
- **1 cup rice, cooked**
- **2 apples, peeled and grated**
- **⅓ lb farmer's cheese, grated**
- **2 tbsp sugar**
- **1 egg, beaten**
- **2 tbsp soft butter**
- **1 cup sour cream**

1. Cut off a slice from the top of each beet and scoop out the centre to make a shell. Also remove a thin slice from the bottom of each beet so they will stand upright.

2. Place beets on a parchment lined tray.

3. Combine cooked rice, grated apple, and grated cheese. Add egg and butter and mix thoroughly.

4. Fill each beet with the rice mixture, and top with sour cream.

5. Bake at 350°F for about 40 minutes.

6. Serve with more sour cream, if desired.

Serves 5.

Beets with Sweet-Sour Sauce

Beets are traditionally associated with Ukrainian cookery, and for good reason – not least of all because beets form the basis of Ukraine's national soup, borshch. Many other cultures enjoy the taste and health benefits of beets as well, and have their own unique preparation methods. The cream in this sauce lends a uniquely Ukrainian flavour to this recipe.

- **2 tbsp butter, melted**
- **2 tbsp flour**
- **½ cup water**
- **¼ cup vinegar**
- **¼ cup whipping cream**
- **¼ cup sugar**
- **½ tsp salt**
- **¼ tsp pepper**
- **6 medium beets, cooked and sliced**

1. Melt butter in a saucepan over medium heat and add flour.
2. Cook until bubbly, stirring constantly.
3. Stir in water and cook until thick, stirring constantly.
4. Mix in vinegar, cream, sugar and seasonings and cook until thick, about 4 minutes, stirring constantly.
5. Pour over beets.

Serves 4.

Tip: Using good quality, thick cream will ensure that you will have no worries about the sauce curdling.

Braised Cabbage

Cabbage and onions are an irresistible combination of flavours. Cook the onion first until very tender. This is the secret to imparting the additional unique sweetness of the onions.

- **1 small head cabbage, shredded**

- **1 large onion, chopped or sliced thinly**

- **5 tbsp butter or oil**

- **Salt and freshly ground pepper**

1. Melt butter in a skillet over medium-low heat.

2. Add onion, season with salt and pepper, and cook slowly until tender.

3. Add cabbage and cook over medium-low heat, stirring occasionally, until cabbage softens.

4. Lower heat and cover, cooking until cabbage begins to brown but is still slightly crisp.

Serves 6.

Brussels Sprouts with Chestnuts

Chestnut trees abound in Ukraine, so it's not surprising that chestnuts are used in many Ukrainian dishes, sweet and savoury, in combination with other vegetables, and in basic bread stuffings and desserts. This dish is a classic and quite easy to prepare. To make it ultra-easy, purchase ready-cooked and peeled chestnuts (available in most supermarkets and specialty food stores). Wedges of savoy cabbage can be substituted for brussels sprouts, with equally delicious results.

- **1 cup chestnuts**
- **3 cups brussels sprouts**
- **3 tbsp butter**
- **3 tbsp flour**
- **1½ cups chicken or beef stock**
- **½ cup browned, buttered bread crumbs**
- **Salt to taste**

1. Cut slits in the shell of each chestnut, cover with boiling water and cook 20 minutes.

2. Cool, remove shells and skins and slice the nuts.

3. Remove any wilted outer leaves from the brussels sprouts and trim the base.

4. Cook sprouts in boiling water to barely cover for about 12 minutes and drain.

5. Melt the butter, stir in the flour and then the stock. Cook, stirring until the sauce thickens. Season with salt to taste.

6. Combine the sauce, sprouts and chestnuts, and simmer for 10 minutes to blend flavors.

7. Garnish with bread crumbs.

Serves 6.

Carrot Loaf

You may have heard that carrots are more nutritious cooked than raw. It's actually true (except when juiced). Because raw carrots have tough cellular walls, the body is able to convert less than 25 per cent of their beta carotene into vitamin A. Cooking, however, frees up nutrients by breaking down the cell membranes. Cooking also increases the antioxidants present in carrots. And a recent study revealed that the antioxidant power of cooked carrots is significantly higher than in raw carrots. However, it's a good idea to eat them in both forms, as cooking destroys the beneficial enzymes found in raw foods. So enjoy your carrots raw (or straight out of the garden!) as well as cooked in dishes like this luscious loaf.

- **2 lbs carrots, grated (about 5 cups)**
- **1 cup bread crumbs**
- **5 tbsp butter**
- **½ cup sour cream**
- **3 large eggs, separated**
- **2 tbsp sugar**
- **2 tbsp flour**
- **1 tsp salt**

1. Mix carrots with bread crumbs and brown in three tablespoons of the melted butter.
2. Remove from heat, blend sour cream, egg yolks, sugar, 2 tablespoons melted butter, flour and salt.
3. Add to carrots.
4. Whip egg whites, add to carrots and mix in well.
5. Place mixture in a well-greased loaf pan and bake at 350°F for 50-60 min.
6. Serve with dollop of sour cream.

Serves 5.

Tip: Antioxidants are located in the skin of fruits and vegetables, so don't peel, but scrub them instead.

Carrot Pancakes

Carrots are one of the most popular vegetables in Ukraine, where there are many ways to prepare them. These unique pancakes are delicious served with sour cream.

- **2 lbs carrots, sliced**
- **5 tbsp butter**
- **1 cup flour**
- **1 large egg**
- **2 tbsp sugar**
- **1 cup sour cream**
- **Salt to taste**

1. Brown carrots in butter and a little water to prevent burning.
2. Cool, then puree or mash.
3. Stir in flour, egg, salt and sugar.
4. Form mixture into pancakes and fry in butter on both sides, until golden brown.
5. Serve with a dollop of sour cream.

Serves 6-8.

Cabbage Pancakes

Good recipes deserve to be shared! I've had this special cabbage pancake recipe for a long, long time. Yet in all my travels and research of recipes, I've only found two recipes for cabbage pancakes. So I thought it was time to share my recipe with you. It is worth a try, as the flavor is outstanding.

You can make them up ahead of time and reheat gently in the oven when you're ready to serve them. They are also delicious cold.

- **1 small cabbage, shredded**
- **4 tbsp butter, vegetable oil or bacon fat**
- **½ cup milk**
- **1 egg yolk**
- **1 whole egg**
- **1 cup flour**
- **½ tsp salt**

1. In a large frying pan, sauté the cabbage in the fat. Season with salt and pepper to taste.

2. For the batter, combine the milk, egg, and egg yolk. Stir mixture into the flour, add the salt, and beat until smooth.

3. Add cabbage to the batter, mixing well.

4. Drop mixture by spoonfuls onto a well greased, medium-hot frying pan or griddle, and fry over medium heat like pancakes. If you find the batter too thick, thin with some soda water, or a little more milk.

5. Serve with sour cream or gravy.

Serves 4-6.

Tip: An easy way to shred the cabbage, if you are not using a mandoline or a box grater, is to cut the cabbage in quarters, remove the core and shred each quarter very finely.

Spinach Patties

Ukrainians have many delicious ways to prepare spinach. Here's just one of them! Great with a tomato or mushroom sauce.

- **2 cups cooked spinach**
- **3 tbsp grated onion**
- **3 tbsp butter**
- **1 large egg, slightly beaten**
- **1 tbsp thick cream**
- **1 cup soft bread crumbs**
- **Salt & freshly ground pepper**

Coating:
- **1 large egg, slightly beaten**
- **1 tbsp water**
- **Fine bread crumbs for dipping**
- **Butter for frying**

1. Squeeze the spinach of excess liquid and chop very finely.

2. Drain the liquid from the grated onion and cook in the butter until very soft.

3. Add the egg, cream, soft bread crumbs and seasoning to the spinach. Blend well. Let rest 8-10 minutes.

4. Shape the mixture into small patties.

5. Dip patties in the fine bread crumbs, slightly beaten egg diluted with one tablespoon water, and back again in the bread crumbs.

6. Pan fry in hot butter until delicately browned on both sides.

Serves 4.

Tip: For moister patties, use soft bread crumbs rather than dry. Make soft bread crumbs by pulsing pieces of fresh bread in the food processor.

Quick Homemade Sauerkraut

Sauerkraut is an extremely healthy food. It is low in calories and high in fibre, vitamins C and K. Medical studies have shown that it may prevent breast cancer. Unpasteurized, raw sauerkraut contains more of the probiotic enzymes lactobacilli than yoghurt. Although the high heat required to pasteurize or cook sauerkraut does kill these enzymes, the other health benefits remain. Making your own sauerkraut is actually very easy, and the taste is outstanding.

- **8 cups cabbage, shredded**
- **2 tbsp sugar**
- **2 tbsp pickling salt**
- **2 tbsp vinegar**
- **2-3 whole bay leaves**
- **Sweet red peppers, chopped (optional)**

1. Choose firm heads of cabbage. Remove the outside leaves of the cabbage head, quarter it, and cut out the core.

2. Shred cabbage with a knife, or a shredder.

3. Combine cabbage, sugar, salt and vinegar.

4. Mix thoroughly and put into a crock.

5. Add the bay leaves and chopped pepper.

6. Press down and put a weight on it.

7. Let sour for five days.

8. Pack in freezer containers, seal and freeze.

Makes about 6 cups.

Tip: Be sure you use pickling salt, not regular table salt.

Sauerkraut with Caraway Seed

Sauerkraut (kapusta in Ukrainian) goes well with any number of foods, especially pork and sausage. The caraway seeds add a nice flavour.

- **2 cups sauerkraut, chopped**
- **1 small onion, chopped finely**
- **3 tbsp bacon fat, or oil**
- **1 tsp sugar**
- **¼ cup water**
- **1 tsp caraway seed**
- **Salt and freshly ground pepper**

1. Rinse the sauerkraut in warm water if it tastes too sour.
2. Drain thoroughly.
3. Fry the onion in the fat until tender.
4. Add the remaining ingredients except the salt, as the sauerkraut may be salty enough. Taste and season.
5. Cook, uncovered, until heated thoroughly.

Serves 4-6.

Tip: A delicious variation to this recipe is to cook about half a pound of sliced smoked sausage with the sauerkraut.

Pickled Lettuce

I've always enjoyed a good dill pickle—cucumber, beet, bean, carrot, asparagus, tomato or mushroom. But now I can add pickled lettuce to the list, thanks to Pawlina who shared her family recipe with me.

Pickled lettuce is ridiculously easy to make and really delicious! All you do is put some washed lettuce leaves (leaf lettuce or Romaine) into leftover fermented dill pickle juice. The lettuce wilts and soaks up the flavor quickly. So it will be done in just a day or so.

If you don't have fermented pickle juice it will take a little longer. To make fermented pickles, pack jars with pickling cucumbers, mini greenhouse cukes, or lettuce, along with several springs of fresh dill, 3-4 cloves garlic, water and pickling salt (about 2 tbsp per litre of water).

Secure the jar lid tightly and leave on the counter to ferment for a few days. The longer you leave the pickles fermenting, the more sour they will get. So refrigerate when sour enough for your liking.

Cabbage Tomato Sauté

This dish is especially delicious with pork dishes and is very easy to make. It was a family favourite when I was growing up, and is still one of my very favourite vegetable dishes.

- **1 small cabbage, shredded**
- **1 medium onion, chopped finely**
- **¼ cup butter or bacon fat**
- **3 tbsp water**
- **2 tbsp butter**
- **2 tbsp flour**
- **1 cup diced tomatoes, fresh or canned**
- **1 tbsp sugar, or to taste**
- **2 tbsp sour cream**
- **Salt & freshly ground pepper**
- **Sprinkle of red pepper flakes**

1. Cook the onion in ¼ cup butter in a large frying pan until tender.

2. Add the cabbage and water and cook, uncovered, for about 15 minutes, or until cabbage is tender but still slightly crisp.

3. In another pan, melt 2 tbsp butter, add the flour, stir to blend.

4. Add the tomatoes and sugar. Cook until the sauce thickens.

5. Add sour cream and season to taste. Add red pepper flakes, if desired.

6. Combine the sauce with the cabbage and bring to a boil.

7. Lower heat and simmer for 5 minutes to blend flavours.

Serves 4.

Dried Pidpenky Mushrooms with Gravy

Dried mushrooms add a unique and intense flavour to any dish and a particularly rich depth to gravies. One of the most popular varieties of wild mushrooms in Ukrainian cuisine is pidpenky.

My sister Leone has fond childhood memories of Mom picking pidpenky on the boulevard in front of our home. Mom would put the mushrooms into a pot of ice-cold water, and Leone would pick out the cleaned mushrooms, which Mom would later cook for us to devour or dry for future use.

There simply is no flavour that matches this delectable mushroom. The closest match to dried pidpenky is probably dried porcini mushrooms. Fortunately, they are available in most supermarkets. Enjoy some in this delicious gravy.

- **2 cups dried mushrooms, pidpenky (or porcini)**
- **1 small onion, chopped finely**
- **1-2 cloves garlic, mashed**
- **6 tbsp oil**
- **4 tbsp browned flour**
- **4 cups hot water**
- **½ tsp salt, or to taste**
- **Freshly ground pepper, to taste**

1. Soak the mushrooms in warm water for half an hour. Drain.
2. Sauté the onion in oil until very soft.
3. Add the garlic and cook for about a minute.
4. Sprinkle the browned flour over the onion. Add the hot water. Stir to make a smooth paste.
5. Add the mushrooms with the salt and pepper.
6. Simmer for about 20 minutes, stirring occasionally.

Makes about 4 cups.

Tip: To brown flour, simply fry white flour in a dry, hot frying pan. Stir constantly until the flour turns a deep golden brown colour.

Beans in Mushroom Sauce

This recipe for beans in mushroom sauce is one of the tastiest ways of eating white beans. It is easy to make, economical and so healthy.

- **4 tbsp flour**
- **4 tbsp oil**
- **1 onion, finely chopped**
- **2 to 3 cloves of garlic, mashed**
- **1 cup water**
- **1 cup sliced mushrooms**
- **1 cup cooked white beans or one 14-15 oz can white beans, drained**
- **Salt and freshly ground pepper**

1. Brown the flour in a heavy skillet over medium heat, stirring constantly to avoid scorching.

2. When the flour turns a dark tan colour, add the oil. Turn temperature to low and stir until smooth.

3. Add the onion and garlic and cook for 5 minutes.

4. Gradually add the water, stirring to avoid lumps.

5. Add the mushrooms and beans, mix well and cook until the mushrooms are tender.

6. Season to taste.

Serves 4.

Eggplant Odesa

Eggplants grow in abundance in the regions of southern Ukraine. There are many sizes and colours of eggplant, which actually is a fruit, specifically a berry. The appearance of the egg shaped white eggplant makes it clear how this fruit was named.

Eggplant is not only nutritious, it also contains a substance that inhibits the rise of cholesterol induced by fatty foods. It works best when not eaten alone, but with cholesterol containing foods.

Eggplant Odesa is a great side dish for the dinner table, or simply with a rustic bread and a salad for a lovely light lunch. It also makes a tasty appetizer or dip.

- **1 large eggplant**
- **1 medium onion, finely chopped**
- **1 large tomato, peeled and finely chopped**
- **2 cloves, garlic, minced**
- **3 tbsp olive oil**
- **2 tbsp red wine vinegar or lemon juice**
- **Salt and freshly ground black pepper to taste**
- **Chopped fresh flat leaf parsley for garnish**

1. Preheat the oven to 375°F.

2. Pierce the eggplant with a knife in several places.

3. Bake for about 50 minutes or until soft on a parchment paper lined baking sheet, turning midway through.

4. Cool and cut the eggplant lengthwise in half. Scoop out the pulp and finely chop or mash.

5. Add the remaining ingredients and mix well.

6. Cover and refrigerate for several hours to allow the flavors to develop.

7. Garnish with chopped parsley.

Serves 4.

Potatoes with Dill Sauce

The sauce in this recipe is equally delicious on other vegetables such as carrots, fish (particularly salmon), and any other dish that lends itself to a savoury herb sauce.

- **2 lbs potatoes**
- **2 tbsp butter**
- **2 tbsp flour**
- **1 cup chicken stock**
- **½ cup whipping cream**
- **1 tbsp chopped fresh dill**
- **Salt to taste**

1. Boil potatoes in salted water with skins on, until fork tender.

2. Drain, cool, peel and slice thick. Set aside.

3. Melt butter in a saucepan over medium heat, add flour and cook a minute.

4. Add chicken stock and cook until thickened.

5. Add cream, dill, and salt.

6. Pour over the potatoes and enjoy!

Serves 6.

Creamy New Potatoes

A special rich and creamy dish my Mom used to make using tiny new nugget potatoes and dill from her own garden. A tender, delicious dish!

- **12 small new potatoes**
- **1 cup cream (approximately)**
- **½ cup chopped dill**

1. Wash and cut potatoes in half.

2. Put them in a casserole, season with salt and pepper and pour in enough cream to almost cover them.

3. Mix in chopped dill.

4. Cover and bake in hot oven (375°F) until forktender (about 35 minutes).

Serves 4.

Creamed Turnips

Here's a simple but delicious way to serve turnip, Ukrainian style. Carrots can be substituted in this recipe for equally delectable results.

- **3 cups cooked turnip, sliced**

- **3 tbsp butter**

- **3 tbsp thick sour cream**

- **1 tbsp flat leaf parsley, chopped**

- **Salt & freshly ground pepper**

1. Sauté turnip slices in butter until turnip begins to brown.

2. Add sour cream and cook a few minutes.

3. Add parsley, salt and pepper to taste.

Serves 6.

Elegant Creamed Carrots

Cream has a way of bringing out flavour in any number of foods. Anyone who has tasted this elegant old country dish will tell you that it makes "eating your vegetables" a delectable treat.

- **7 medium carrots, sliced**
- **5 tbsp butter**
- **2 tbsp flour**
- **4 tbsp sugar, or to taste**
- **½ cup sweet cream**
- **Salt**
- **Fresh dill for garnish (optional)**

1. Cook sliced carrots (in enough water to cover) over medium heat, until tender. Drain.

2. Make a roux of the butter and flour, but do not brown.

3. Add cream, salt and sugar, and mix well.

4. Add carrots and cook 5-6 minutes.

5. Garnish with fresh dill springs, or chopped dill, if desired.

Serves 4-6.

Green Bean Bake

Something about the combination of bacon, onion and beans makes this dish hard to resist. This recipe calls for green (string) beans but you can substitute different varieties, such as lima beans, broad beans, kidney beans, black beans, navy beans, yellow wax beans—the choice is yours.

- **4 thin slices bacon, diced**

- **1 small onion, finely chopped**

- **1 cup mushrooms, sliced**

- **2 cups green beans, cooked**

- **1 cup tomato juice**

- **2 tbsp thick sour cream**

- **Salt & freshly ground pepper**

1. Fry the bacon until crisp.

2. Add the onion and cook until tender.

3. Combine with the mushrooms and the remaining ingredients.

4. Place the mixture into a baking dish, cover and bake for 30 minutes at 375°F.

Serves 4.

Tip: Always fry bacon on low heat to extract as much of the fat as possible and avoid scorching it.

Mixed Winter Root Vegetables

Root vegetables are so versatile! We roast, bake, fry in oil and steam them. I don't think we ever get tired of them, which is a good thing as they are so healthy for us and the recipes are endless.

The parsnip (petrushka in Ukrainian) is a wonderful root vegetable that is too often overlooked. Parsnips look like thick, white carrots and have a delightfully sweet, nutty flavor. They are available most of the year, but are best in the colder months, as they sweeten after the first frost.

Parsnip wedges can be cooked with roast beef, added during the last hour of cooking. Or, add slices to soups and stews in the last 30 minutes of cooking. They are great puréed with mashed potatoes, or baked apples. They are also good roasted on their own with brown sugar, butter and nutmeg.

This combination of parsnip roasted with other root vegetables is a real winner! Serve with your favourite meat dish.

- **1 medium turnip**
- **1 large parsnip, sliced**
- **2 large carrots, sliced**
- **2 large potatoes, quartered**
- **¼ cup butter**
- **½ cup boiling water**
- **1 teaspoon salt, or to taste**

1. Melt butter in boiling water.
2. Place the veggies in a casserole, pour the melted butter and water over them, and sprinkle with salt.
3. Cover and bake in a 375° oven for about 1 ½ hours, without turning or removing the lid.

Serves 4.

Honey Roasted Root Vegetables

Honey enhances the natural sweetness of root vegetables and creates a lovely glaze. This recipe is equally at home served at a simple family supper or at an elegant dinner party.

- **½ cup honey**
- **3 tbsp butter, softened**
- **1½ lbs parsnips, turnips, or carrots, diced**

1. Mix honey and butter and pour over vegetables.

2. Roast at 375°F until tender, turning a few times to coat all sides.

Serves 4.

Tip: Buy smaller parsnips if possible. If using large ones, split in half and remove the woody core.

Cakes & Tortes

Poppy Seed Cake

This cake freezes very well. It's like a coffee cake, very good for breakfast or with fruit for a dessert. Excellent with a rum or lemon sauce.

- **1 cup poppy seed**
- **1 cup milk**
- **1 cup butter**
- **2 cups sugar**
- **3 large eggs, separated**
- **2 cups flour**
- **½ tsp salt**
- **2½ tsp double acting baking powder**
- **2 tsp vanilla**
- **Icing sugar**

1. Put poppy seed in milk, bring to a boil, and set aside for an hour.

2. Preheat oven to 350°F.

3. Cream butter and sugar until fluffy. Beat in egg yolks. Add poppy seed and milk mixture.

4. Sift flour, salt and baking powder together, and stir into poppy seed and milk mixture. Mix well.

5. Beat egg white until stiff, beat in vanilla, and fold into batter with a spatula or wire whisk.

6. Grease a large loaf pan with butter. Sprinkle flour over bottom and sides, fill pan with batter and bake 1 hour, or until done.

7. Invert on a rack to cool. Just before serving, sprinkle icing sugar on top of cake.

Makes 1 loaf.

Spiced Honey Cake

Medivnyk and medyannyk are two names commonly used for Ukrainian honey cake. Both names stem from the Ukrainian word med or mead, which means honey. Plain or fruit medivynyk is the traditional Ukrainian Christmas and New Year cake. It's a good idea to make this cake a few days ahead to give it time to ripen. This cake is freezer friendly.

- **1 cup honey, melted**
- **4 large eggs, separated**
- **1 cup sugar**
- **4 tbsp oil**
- **1 cup tea or coffee**
- **1 tsp baking soda**
- **3 cups flour**
- **1 tsp baking powder**
- **½ tsp salt**
- **1 tsp cinnamon**
- **1 tsp allspice**
- **½ tsp nutmeg**
- **1 cup walnuts, chopped**

1. Bring the honey to a boil. Cool.

2. Beat the egg yolks until light and fluffy. Beat in the oil, honey, and sugar.

3. Combine the tea, or coffee, with baking soda.

4. Sift the dry ingredients then add, alternating with tea or coffee, to the egg mixture.

5. Stir in the walnuts.

6. Beat the egg whites until stiff and fold into the batter.

7. Grease a 9x13 inch cake pan.

8. Pour mixture into pan and bake at 325°F for 50 to 55 minutes, or until cake tester comes out clean.

Serves 8-10.

Quick Honey Cake

This modern adaptation of a traditional recipe is lovely served with a lemon glaze, or a dollop of sour cherry preserves mixed with sour cream. To make the glaze, just add enough fresh lemon juice to 1 cup sifted icing sugar to make a glaze you can drizzle. Serve with rum or honey sauce, whipped cream, or ice cream. For extra-special events, decorate with marzipan honey bees. Or, serve the honey cake with fresh cut flowers or a beeswax candle in the centre.

- **3 large eggs, room temperature**
- **1 cup sugar**
- **1 cup honey**
- **1 cup corn or olive oil**
- **3 cups sifted flour**
- **1 tsp baking soda**
- **2 tsp baking powder**
- **1 tsp cinnamon**
- **1 cup milk**

1. Beat eggs with mixer, gradually adding sugar, until light.
2. Blend in honey, then oil, blending well with each addition.
3. Sift dry ingredients together.
4. Add flour mixture alternately with milk to egg-honey mixture, mixing until well blended.
5. Bake in a greased and floured angel food cake pan, or a 12-cup bundt pan, at 325°F or 60-70 minutes, or until an inserted tester comes out clean.

Serves 10-12.

Tip: Honey cakes can burn easily so make sure oven temperature does not exceed 325°F.

Sour Cream Cake

In the days before pasteurization and refrigeration, cream which was soured was not thrown away but used by Ukrainians and other East Europeans to flavor dishes such as borshch, beef stroganoff, and paprika flavored dishes such as goulash. Known as smetana, sour cream is now commercially produced and is used in a wide variety of dishes, from appetizers to main dishes and desserts. Sour cream adds a delectable moistness to this cake.

- ¾ cup butter
- 1½ cups sugar
- 3 eggs
- 1½ cups sour cream, full fat (14%)
- 1 tsp baking powder
- 1½ tsp baking soda
- 2½ cups flour

Filling:
- ¾ cup sugar
- 2 tsp cinnamon
- ½ cup chopped walnuts

1. Cream butter and sugar until fluffy.
2. Add the eggs and sour cream, mixing to blend.
3. Add sifted dry ingredients.
4. Pour half the batter in a 9x9 inch greased pan.
5. Cover with the filling then add the rest of the batter.
6. Bake in a 350°F oven for 45 minutes, or until cake tester comes out clean.

Serves 8.

Hutsul Apple Cake

A few years ago, the chef at a hotel I was staying at in the Hutsul area of the Carpathian Mountains in western Ukraine prepared this beautiful Ukrainian apple cake for my birthday party dinner. It was exquisite! This recipe is similar, and also works well with pitted cherries, plums, or sliced peaches or pears. Lovely served with slightly sweetened whipped cream or ice cream.

- 1½ cups flour
- ¼ cup sugar
- ¼ tsp salt
- 2 tsp baking powder
- ⅓ cup butter
- 1 large egg, well beaten
- ½ cup cream
- 4 tart apples, thinly sliced
- ½ cup sugar
- 2 tsp cinnamon

1. Sift together flour, sugar, salt and baking powder. Cut in butter until mixture is crumbly.

2. Combine egg with cream and stir into the flour mixture. Mix lightly, handling the dough as little as possible.

3. Pat dough into a buttered 8x8 inch baking pan.

4. Pare the apples. Slice very thinly and spread over the dough.

5. Mix the sugar and cinnamon and sprinkle over apples. Dot with butter.

6. Bake at 350°F for 25 minutes or until fruit is tender.

Serves 6.

Rhubarb Cake

Rhubarb is indigenous to Asia, and has been used for its medicinal qualities for thousands of years. It grows wild in Ukraine, where it very likely was introduced by Mongol Tatars during their 12th and 13th century raids. Ancients valued rhubarb's strong laxative and astringent quality, and a roaring rhubarb trade existed between Europe and Asia for centuries. Modern medicine is starting to catch up; the British journal *Nature* recently reported that rhubarb is a high-powered medicine akin to aspirin and penicillin.

Rhubarb was not used as a food until sugar became widely and inexpensively available. Today, the tart stems of this plant (the leaves are poisonous) are used in many European or Asian cuisines including, of course, Ukrainian. My mom grew rhubarb in her garden, and used it to make divinely delicious desserts like this cake.

- **2 large eggs, beaten**
- **1¼ cups sugar**
- **1 cup sour cream, 14% butterfat**
- **1 tsp baking soda**
- **½ tsp salt**
- **2 cups flour**
- **2½ cups fresh rhubarb, chopped**

Topping:
- **1 cup sugar**
- **¼ cup butter**
- **¼ cup flour**

1. Mix eggs, sugar and sour cream thoroughly.
2. Add in rhubarb and dry ingredients. Mix well.
3. Pour into a 9x13 inch well-greased and floured pan.
4. Mix topping ingredients until crumbly. Cover cake batter.
5. Bake at 350°F for 45 minutes.

Serves 12.

Rhubarb Almond Cake

One of the first signs of spring in our gardens is finding rhubarb growing. Rhubarb is technically a vegetable, although most of us think of rhubarb as a fruit. It's easy to grow and it will come back every year because it is a perennial.

Mom and Dad had a large rhubarb plant in their garden, and every spring Mom would make something delicious with rhubarb, usually a compote, pie or cake. So celebrate spring (or any season or reason) by making this scrumptious cake. It's a winner!

- **2 cups flour**
- **1 tsp soda**
- **¼ tsp salt**
- **1 ½ cups brown sugar**
- **½ cup butter**
- **1 egg**
- **1 cup milk**
- **1 tsp vanilla**
- **2½ cups rhubarb, diced**

Topping:
- **¼ cup sugar**
- **1 tsp cinnamon**
- **½ cup sliced almonds**

1. Mix together flour, soda and salt. Set aside.

2. In another bowl, cream brown sugar with butter. Add egg, milk, and vanilla and beat.

3. Gradually add dry ingredients to creamed ingredients, mixing thoroughly.

4. Mix in the rhubarb.

5. Pour into a greased 9x13 inch pan.

6. Mix sugar, cinnamon and almonds together. Sprinkle over top of the batter.

7. Bake at 350° for 40 minutes or until a tester comes out clean.

8. Serve with whipped cream or a scoop of vanilla ice cream.

Serves 8-10.

Chocolate Honey Cake

The abundance of honey in Ukraine inspired cooks to experiment with honey baking in the past, when sugar was not known. Remember all honey cakes and honey cookies require a few days to ripen, so the flavors develop. In the following recipe for chocolate honey cake, a blend of honey and chocolate makes this cake rich, tender, moist, flavorful and fine textured.

You could serve this cake simply topped with a layer of raspberry preserves and sprinkled with chocolate shavings or topped with chocolate icing.

- **3 oz or squares of unsweetened chocolate, melted**
- **⅔ cup liquid honey**
- **1 ¾ cup sifted cake flour**
- **1 tsp baking soda**
- **½ tsp baking powder**
- **½ tsp salt**
- **½ cup butter**
- **⅔ cup sugar**
- **1 tsp vanilla**
- **2 eggs**
- **⅔ cup sour milk or buttermilk**

1. Melt the chocolate, add the honey and blend well. Cool to lukewarm.

2. Sift the flour, baking powder, baking soda and salt.

3. Cream the butter and sugar until light and fluffy.

4. Stir in the vanilla and beat eggs in one at a time. Blend in the chocolate honey mixture.

5. Add in the flour alternately with the sour milk or buttermilk.

6. Butter an 8 by 8 inch baking pan and bake at 350°F for 20 minutes.

7. Lower the temperature to 325°F to avoid burning and bake another 20 minutes or until done when tested.

Serves 8-10.

Summer Fruit Cake

This delectable and easy-to-make summer fruit cake will become one of your favorite summer cake recipes.

- **3 cups flour**
- **1 cup sugar**
- **1 cup butter**
- **½ tsp baking soda**
- **2 tbsp water**
- **1 cup sour cream**
- **1 egg**
- **1 lb berries or 2 lbs fruit**
- **1 cup icing sugar**
- **2-3 tbsp flour (optional)**

1. Cream the butter and sugar until fluffy.

2. Add mixed flour and soda and blend in well.

3. Add the water, sour cream and slightly beaten egg and blend thoroughly.

4. Roll the dough on a slightly floured surface into a circle about 9 inches in diameter, and place it into a buttered 9-inch round cake pan.

5. Arrange fruit in a layer on top of the dough—strawberries, raspberries, blueberries or cherries; pitted and cut plums or thinly sliced, pitted peaches or apricots.

6. Sprinkle the fruit or berries with icing sugar. If the berries are really juicy, mix 2-3 tablespoons of flour in with the icing sugar.

7. Bake at 350°F for 45 minutes. Cool and serve.

Serves 8-10.

Strawberry Cake Roll

While this recipe does not have ancient roots in Ukrainian folklore, it has become popular in modern Ukrainian cuisine.

- **2 large eggs**
- **¾ cup sugar**
- **1 cup flour**
- **1 tsp tsp baking powder**
- **¼ tsp baking soda**
- **⅛ tsp salt**
- **⅓ cup sour cream**

Filling:
- **1 cup of strawberries, sliced or crushed**
- **¼ cup icing sugar**
- **1 cup whipping cream**
- **Whole sugared strawberries for garnish**

1. Preheat over to 400°F.

2. Beat the eggs and sugar until thick and pale. Fold in the dry sifted ingredients and sour cream.

3. Line a baking sheet with parchment paper and spread batter over it evenly.

4. Bake at 400°F for 12 minutes or until cake is golden and springs back when touched.

5. Turn cake onto a kitchen towel that has been dusted with icing sugar. Remove parchment paper. Cool the cake slightly and then roll it up tightly with the towel, jelly roll fashion. Let cool completely.

6. Whip cream and fold in icing sugar and strawberries.

7. Unroll the cake and spread with the strawberries and whipped cream. Gently roll up and chill 1 hour.

8. Slice and scatter with sugared whole strawberries.

Serves 8-10.

Tip: If you don't have fresh strawberries on hand, spread a thin layer of strawberry jam over the cake and top with whipped cream before rolling up.

Elegant Walnut Torte

This elegant, old-world dessert is absolutely delectable and perfect for any occasion. It takes a bit of effort, but is well worth it!

- **5 large eggs, separated**
- **½ cup butter, room temperature**
- **1 cup sugar**
- **1 cup walnuts, ground**
- **½ cup milk**
- **2 cups flour**
- **2 tsp baking powder**
- **1 tsp salt**
- **Fine bread crumbs**

Walnut Butter Cream:

- **2 cups butter**
- **1 cup icing sugar**
- **1 cup canned milk, unsweetened**
- **½ cup ground walnuts**
- **½ tsp walnut, vanilla or maple extract**
- **12 halves walnuts for garnish**

1. Preheat oven to 350°F. Butter a 10-inch round cake pan and dust with fine bread crumbs.

2. Sift together flour, baking powder and salt.

3. Cream butter, sugar and egg yolks together until light and fluffy. Add ground walnuts and milk, mixing well. Then blend in dry ingredients.

4. Beat egg whites until stiff, then gently fold into butter mixture. Pour batter into the cake pan and bake 30 minutes or until done.

5. Rest for five minutes before removing from pan. Chill thoroughly before applying the butter cream.

6. To make the butter cream, mix butter and sugar until creamy.

7. Add milk, gradually blending in two tablespoons at a time, mixing well between each addition. Set aside 1 cup. Add ground walnuts and extract to the rest of the mixture.

8. Cut cake into 3 or 4 layers. Spread butter cream on each layer, leaving enough to cover the top. Stack layers.

9. Fill an icing bag with the 1 cup reserved butter mixture and use a star or rose tip to make 12 bases for the walnut halves.

Serves 12.

Walnut Almond Torte

Organic whipping cream has a slightly higher fat content so it beats up better, which also makes it ideal for piping.

- **1 cup butter**
- **½ cup icing sugar**
- **¼ lb ground almonds (1¼ cups)**
- **2 cups flour**

Filling:

- **1 lb ground walnuts (4½ cups)**
- **1 cup icing sugar**
- **½ cup cream**
- **1 cup whipping cream**
- **1 tsp vanilla**

1. Cream butter and sugar until light and fluffy.

2. Mix in ground almonds and flour until blended. Divide dough into four parts.

3. Place each portion into 4 greased 8 inch layer cake pans, and spread to edges of each pan.

4. Bake at 350°F until golden, about 12 to 15 minutes. Cool and remove from pan.

5. Mix the ground walnuts, icing sugar and enough cream to moisten. Divide filling into 3 equal amounts and spread over three layers, stacking on top of each other and topping with the fourth.

6. Whip remaining cream with vanilla. Refrigerate.

7. One hour before serving, spread vanilla whipped cream over top and sides. Decorate with chocolate swirls. Refrigerate until serving.

Serves 10.

Meringue Torte

This recipe calls for strawberries, but other seasonal fruits such as raspberries or blueberries can be used with equally delicious results. For a nice variation add ½ cup sifted cocoa to the whipping cream.

- **6 large egg whites, room temperature**

- **½ tsp cream of tartar**

- **2 cups berry or superfine sugar**

Filling and topping:
- **2 cups strawberries, sliced**

- **1 tbsp sugar**

- **3½ cups heavy whipping cream**

- **⅓ cup granulated sugar**

- **1 tsp vanilla**

- **12 whole strawberries**

1. Beat egg whites with cream of tartar until frothy. Add sugar, one tablespoon at a time and continue beating until all the sugar is used and stiff peaks are formed.

2. Line a baking tray with two 9-inch circles of parchment paper. Spoon meringue onto parchment circles. Raise the edges of the meringue circles slightly with the back of the spoon until stiff peaks are formed.

3. Bake at 275°F for 1 hour or longer. Cakes should be dry. Turn off oven and leave cakes in until oven has cooled.

4. Combine sliced strawberries and 1 tablespoon sugar in a small bowl and let stand 30 minutes. Drain any accumulated juices.

5. Beat cream, remaining sugar and vanilla in a large bowl until firm peaks form. Gently fold sliced strawberries into whipped cream.

6. Fill bottom cake with some filling. Place second cake on top. Cover top and sides with remaining filling. Garnish with whole strawberries.

Serves 10-12.

Tip: Make individual meringues by heaping spoonfuls of meringue into 3-inch circles on a parchment-lined baking tray. Hollow out centers with the back of a spoon to hold the filling. Bake as directed.

Prune Torte

When I was growing up, we always had sweets made with prunes and plums, especially for wedding showers. I've had the recipe for this outstanding torte for so long that I really don't remember where it came from. It's very easy to make and freezes well. Low in fat but high in fibre and flavour, it only tastes rich and decadent!

- 1½ cups prunes
- 2 cups flour
- 2½ cups sugar
- 1 tsp baking soda
- 1 tsp cinnamon
- ½ tsp nutmeg
- ½ tsp ground cloves
- 3 large eggs, beaten
- 1 cup oil
- 1 cup buttermilk
- ½ tsp soda

1. To cook prunes, add water just to cover. Cook over medium heat until softened, about 4-5 minutes. Cool.

2. Sift dry ingredients together. Add oil and beaten eggs, mixing thoroughly.

3. Mix ½ tsp soda into the buttermilk, add to batter, along with prunes.

4. Pour into two 9-inch round layer cake pans, or three 8-inch pans lined with parchment paper.

5. Bake at 350°F for 45 minutes or until tester inserted into cake (not prunes) comes out dry. Cake should be a light golden colour.

6. Fill and ice with your favourite icing (chocolate is nice) or a lemon or rum glaze. For an even more intense fruit flavour, fill with povydlo (plum butter) or thick plum jam.

Makes one two-layer torte.

Tip: Parchment paper makes for easy removal of any type of fruit cake.

Cherry and Walnut Slice

Cherries and nuts of all kinds are common in Ukrainian pastries. This lovely slice will satisfy any sweet tooth.

- **1½ cup pastry flour**
- **½ cup white sugar**
- **1 tsp baking powder**
- **½ cup butter**
- **1 large egg**
- **1 egg yolk**
- **1 egg white**
- **½ cup brown sugar**
- **1 cup walnuts, chopped**
- **1 cup glazed cherries, chopped**

1. Sift flour, add sugar and baking powder and blend.

2. Rub in butter, mix in unbeaten egg and egg yolk.

3. Spread in greased 8 inch square pan.

4. Beat egg white until stiff, add brown sugar, walnuts and cherries. Spread over base layer.

5. Bake at 350°F for 45 minutes.

Serves 16.

Tip: Pastry flour gives a more tender product, but regular all-purpose flour works, too.

Sweet Fancy Nalysnyky

These nalysnyky are different from the crepe-like variety that are rolled. These fine-textured cakes are stacked, with a variety of fillings between them. For a particularly elegant presentation, try a honey filling and cover in meringue. Crushed, sweetened fruit or thick jam laced with a bit of brandy or rum also lend themselves wonderfully to this unique, traditional dessert.

- **1 tbsp butter, softened**
- **2 tbsp sugar**
- **¼ tsp salt**
- **3 large eggs, separated**
- **¼ cup flour**
- **¼ cup milk**
- **¼ cup water**
- **1 tsp vanilla**

1. Cream the butter, sugar and salt.

2. Beat egg yolks until light. Add to butter-sugar mixture, and beat until smooth.

3. Add flour, milk and water. Beat thoroughly. Stir in vanilla.

4. Beat egg whites until stiff and fold into the batter.

5. In a non-stick crepe pan, pour ½ cup (4 oz.) of batter into the centre of the pan. Fry over medium-low heat, browning lightly on both sides. (Cakes are delicate so handle gently.) Repeat 4 times for a total of 5 cakes.

6. Spread each cake with desired filling and stack in a buttered baking dish. For an elegant touch, cover with meringue. (Recipe on next page.)

7. Serve warm or at room temperature.

Serves 6.

Tip: Always use pure rather than artificial vanilla extract. Pure vanilla is more expensive, but its flavour is smoother, sweeter, and more intense, so you need less of it for the same result.

Honey Filling for Sweet Fancy Nalysnyky

The meringue topping adds a beautiful decorative finish to this unusual and elegant dessert.

Honey Filling:
- **3 tbsp butter**
- **½ cup honey**
- **½ tsp grated lemon or orange rind**
- **1 tsp each lemon and orange juice**
- **½ cup walnuts, ground or finely chopped**

Meringue:
- **3 large egg whites, room temperature**
- **3 tbsp sugar**
- **½ tsp vanilla**

1. Cream butter and honey well.

2. Stir in remaining ingredients.

3. Spread filling on each cake layer (see Sweet Fancy Nalysnyky recipe on facing page), as directed, stacking the layers on top of each other.

4. Beat egg whites, gradually adding sugar, until stiff peaks form. Fold in vanilla.

5. Spread meringue over top and sides of the stack of cakes.

6. Brown lightly in a preheated 350°F oven, about 12-15 minutes. Watch carefully to avoid scorching.

7. Remove from oven and dredge with vanilla sugar.

8. Serve warm or at room temperature.

Tip: When beating egg whites, make sure not to over-beat, or they will separate and become watery. Stop beating when stiff peaks form.

Sweets, Treats, & Desserts

Makagigi (Almond Brittle)

Nuts are nutritious and therefore perfect for a sensible sweet snack. In Ukraine, almonds are probably the most widely used nut, although walnuts are also highly prized. Makagigi is an easy-to-make almond brittle that is a traditional favourite in Ukraine. It is also delicious using walnuts.

- ¼ cup sugar

- ½ cup honey

- ⅔ cup butter

- 1 lb blanched almonds or walnuts (about 3 cups), chopped coarsely

1. Melt the sugar in a heavy frying pan over medium heat, until golden.

2. Add the honey and butter and simmer slowly for 20 minutes, stirring gently.

3. Stir in the nuts and cook for another 10 minutes.

4. Oil a cookie sheet and drop the mixture from a tablespoon.

5. Let cool.

Makes 16-18 snacks.

Almond Holiday Balls

Dried, sweetened tart cherries can be used in place of the candied cherries in this recipe.

- **1 cup butter**
- **½ cup icing sugar**
- **2 cups sifted all-purpose flour**
- **1 cup ground almonds**
- **1 tsp vanilla extract**
- **18 halved candied cherries, maraschinos, or dried tart cherries**

1. Cream butter and sugar until light and fluffy.

2. Mix in all the other ingredients, except for cherries, using your hands.

3. Take a tablespoon of dough, start forming it into a ball. Push in half of the cherry and continue to roll in your hands to make a perfect ball.

4. Place on a greased baking sheet.

5. Bake at 325°F for 35 minutes.

6. While still hot, roll the balls in icing sugar.

Makes 36 confections.

Dried Fruit Candy

This candy is a natural treat that is fun and easy to make. It keeps well, too — as long as it's in a secret hiding place where no one can find it! I recommend using the medjool date from California. These dates are plump and soft, with a smooth shiny skin. Top the candy with icing sugar or melted chocolate, dark or light.

- **½ lb prunes, pitted and steamed (2½ cups)**

- **½ lb dates, pitted (1½ cups)**

- **½ lb raisins (1½ cups)**

- **½ lb walnuts or blanched almonds (3¾ cups)**

- **2 tbsp honey**

- **Icing sugar or 2 oz melted chocolate**

1. Put all the dried fruits and nuts in a food processor with the honey.

2. Pulse until mixture is well blended.

3. For balls, shape mixture into small balls. Roll balls in icing sugar.

4. For bars, line a pan with parchment paper. Press mixture into the pan about ¾ inch thick. Spread with the melted chocolate. Let topping set before cutting into bars.

Makes 12 bars.

Tip: To melt chocolate, use a double boiler or a bowl over a pot of just simmering hot water. Definitely not rapidly boiling water!

Nougat

These confections are rich and delicious on their own, but if you want to be really decadent, dip them into melted dipping chocolate after they've cooled.

Honey and walnuts are what make this nougat uniquely Ukrainian. The honey gives it a more robust flavour and a softer, chewier texture. The walnuts give it a distinct taste and texture from nougats using nuts such as almonds and pistachios.

- **1 cup sugar**
- **⅓ cup honey**
- **⅓ cup light corn syrup**
- **¼ cup water**
- **¼ tsp salt**
- **2 egg whites**
- **¼ tsp vanilla**
- **1 cup walnuts or almonds, chopped coarsely**

1. Combine sugar, honey, corn syrup, and water.
2. Cook, stirring only until sugar dissolves (to 260°F).
3. Add salt to egg whites and beat until stiff.
4. Slowly pour syrup over whites, beating constantly until thick.
5. Add vanilla and nuts.
6. Drop from teaspoon on greased baking sheet or pour into a greased pan.
7. Cool and cut into pieces.

Makes 24 pieces.

Kutia

This ancient, traditional dish is made of cooked wheat flavoured with honey, nuts, and ground poppy seeds. Its origins date back ~5000 years, when it appears the Ukrainian people first cultivated wheat. It is the first dish of the 12-course meatless and dairy-less supper served at Christmas Eve and the Feast of Jordan (Epiphany). It is also sometimes served at funerals. If you can't get wheat kernels fresh from the farm, you can find them at most health food stores and in some supermarket bulk food sections.

- **2 cups wheat kernels**
- **Water to cover**
- **Salt to taste**
- **1 cup honey**
- **½ cup poppy seeds**
- **½ cup chopped walnuts (optional)**

1. Soak wheat overnight, in water to cover. The next day, simmer it in the same water, covered, for 4-6 hours. Stir occasionally, or until tender and beginning to burst. Add more water if necessary, and salt to taste.

2. When kernels are done, stir in honey.

3. Scald ½ cup of poppy seeds in water to cover, then drain. Grind in a blender, food chopper, or coffee or nut grinder. (This step is important to get the most flavour.)

4. Add poppy seeds and walnuts to the wheat and honey mixture.

5. Serve warm or cold. It's freezer-friendly and keeps in the refrigerator for about two weeks.

Serves 8-10.

Tip: For best results, use hard spring wheat. Softer varieties, including pearl wheat, will turn mushy.

Uzvar (Christmas Compote)

This traditional dried fruit compote is an enduring component of the Sviat Vechir (Ukrainian Christmas Eve) supper. This compote will keep in the refrigerator for 2 weeks, so it's a great make-ahead.

- **1½ lbs mixed dried fruit (pears, apples, prunes, raisins)**
- **5 cups apple cider**
- **3 tbsp honey**
- **3 tbsp sugar**
- **1 cinnamon stick**
- **5-6 whole cloves**
- **1 whole lemon, zested and juiced**

1. In a non-reactive pot, bring dried fruit and cider to a boil, over medium heat.
2. Add honey, sugar, cloves, and cinnamon stick. Cook until sugar dissolves.
3. Add lemon juice and zest.
4. Simmer, covered, for an hour.
5. Serve warm or chilled in crystal or clear glass bowls.

Serves 6-8.

Pumpkin Rice Pudding

Great as an accompaniment for roasted meats and game as well as for dessert.

- **2 cups milk**

- **1 cup long grain rice**

- **2 tsp salt**

- **2 tbsp butter**

- **2-4 cups pumpkin puree (fresh or canned)**

- **3 tbsp sugar**

- **1 cup seedless raisins**

- **1 cup chopped blanched almonds**

- **¼ tsp almond extract**

- **1 whole pumpkin (preferably with a stem)**

1. Heat milk in a heavy pot. Add rice and salt and bring to a boil, reduce heat, cover and cook 15 minutes.

2. Melt the butter in a skillet, add half the pumpkin puree and sugar.

3. Plump raisins in hot water and then drain. Add raisins, chopped almonds and almond extract to the cooked rice.

4. Cut the top of the pumpkin to make a lid, remove seeds and membrane. Butter the inside generously.

5. Fill with half of the rice mixture, then a layer of pumpkin puree, then lastly the rest of the rice mixture. Dot with butter.

6. Bake at 350°F on a greased heavy baking pan or cookie sheet for one hour or until warmed through. Spoon out filling to serve.

Serves 8.

Tip: Adjust the amount of pumpkin puree to your taste.

Baked Noodle Raisin Dessert

Traditional at Easter, but wonderful any time of the year.

- **3 cups egg noodles**
- **½ cup melted butter**
- **½ cup golden raisins**
- **¼ cup sugar**
- **½ tsp cinnamon**
- **3 large eggs, well beaten**
- **1 cup scalded milk, cooled**
- **Pinch salt**

1. Cook noodles in salted water until almost done. Drain.

2. Add melted butter and mix. Add raisins.

3. Mix salt, sugar, cinnamon, eggs and milk. Add to pasta.

4. Place mixture in a buttered 9x13 inch baking dish.

5. Bake at 350°F for 30 minutes or until golden on top.

Serves 6.

Tip: Because you will also be baking the noodles, make sure to undercook them slightly for this dish so it doesn't end up mushy.

Sweet Millet Pudding

Millet is an ancient grain that is, fortunately for all of us, coming back in vogue. It can be used as a tasty and healthy alternative to rice or quinoa. It has a more distinct, slightly nuttier taste than brown rice, but is milder than quinoa.

This recipe is delicious as a dessert or gourmet breakfast. For a creamier dish, use milk instead of water. If you like, add ½ cup chopped walnuts or almonds. For a lovely variation, substitute dried plums for the dates and add 2 tablespoons sesame seeds.

- **1 cup millet**
- **4 cups water**
- **1 tsp salt**
- **½ cup coconut, fancy**
- **½ cup sunflower seeds**
- **½ cup dates, pitted and chopped**
- **½ cup golden raisins**

1. Rinse millet until water runs clear.

2. Bring millet with water and salt to a boil. Cook until water is absorbed and millet is tender.

3. Add remaining ingredients just before serving.

Serves 6-8.

Cherry Bread Pudding

I find the cherry desserts to be very special because I love both sweet and sour juicy cherries. We had both types of cherry trees in our garden when I was a kid. Our family dog loved the cherries too, even the sour ones.

Dad made beautiful sour cherry wine and mum made all kinds of cherry desserts—pies, cakes, soups, puddings and sweet perogies. She never pitted the cherries as she felt the pits imparted a great flavor. Remember to remind anyone who is devouring this pudding to watch out for the pits—if you have decided to do the same and not pit them for this recipe.

- **2 cups dried regular or sweet bread, diced**
- **1 ½ cups warm milk**
- **3 eggs, separated**
- **½ cup sugar**
- **¼ tsp salt**
- **½ tsp cinnamon**
- **2 tbsp melted butter**
- **1 lb cherries pitted or whole**
- **⅓ cup blanched almonds, chopped**

1. Soak the bread in the milk to soften.

2. Beat egg yolks, sugar and salt. Add the bread and toss. Mix in the cinnamon, melted butter, cherries and almonds. Beat the egg whites until stiff, and fold into the cherry mixture.

3. Put the batter into a buttered baking dish and place it in a pan of hot water. Cover and bake in a 350° oven for about 35 minutes. Serve hot with a dollop of yogurt, vanilla, ice cream, sour cream or sweet cream.

Serves 4-6.

Baked Apples with Red Wine

Apples grow abundantly in Ukraine, with hundreds of varieties grown. Baking apples are best for this elegant dessert, but any variety can be used. Keep in mind, however, that baking times will vary depending on the variety (and the size) of apples used.

- **6 baking apples**
- **6 tbsp strawberry preserves**
- **½ cup walnuts, chopped finely**
- **½ cup sugar**
- **1½ cups red wine**

1. Wash and core apples to about one-half inch from the bottom.

2. Pierce apple skins with a needle or skewer in 6 places to help prevent skin cracking.

3. Mix strawberry preserves with the walnuts and fill the apple centers. Place in a baking dish.

4. Mix the sugar and wine and pour over the apples

5. Bake at 375°F for about 35 minutes or until apples are tender.

6. Baste while baking.

7. Chill and serve with wine syrup and whipped cream, if desired.

Serves 6.

Fresh Berry Compote

Sweets have become a dietary pariah in today's world, along with fats and salt. But there's no reason not to enjoy a sweet treat at the end of a meal once in a while—especially if it's a sensible treat.

Stay away from the empty calories of sugary, fat-laden items and focus instead on sweets with nutritional value. The most obvious, of course, is a piece of fruit, or a dish that uses the natural sweetness of fruit to satisfy your sweet tooth.

Here's a delightful, refreshing, traditional fresh berry compote that is very easy to make.

- **1 lb strawberries or raspberries**
- **1 cup sugar**
- **1 cup water**
- **Brandy or wine for flavouring (optional)**

1. Bring sugar and water to a boil and add to berries.

2. Add wine or brandy.

3. Let stand several hours before serving.

Serves 4.

Sour Cherry Compote

Fresh sour, or Morello, cherries are definitely a Ukrainian favorite, and can be found in many orchards throughout Ukraine. Sour cherries (vyshnia in Ukrainian) make the most wonderful wine, jellies, jams and pies. Lucky for us, dried sour cherries are readily available in most supermarkets, and cans and jars of sour cherries imported from Eastern Europe are available in many specialty shops and delis.

- ¾ **cup dried sour cherries**
- ¾ **cup dried cranberries**
- 1½ **cups water**
- ½ **cup sugar, or to taste**
- ⅛ **tsp almond extract**

1. Simmer the dried fruits with water and sugar in a small heavy saucepan over medium heat, stirring constantly until the fruit is softened, and the liquid is a little syrupy, about 15 minutes.

2. Remove from stove and add the almond extract.

3. Cool and store in the refrigerator until ready to use.

Makes 3 cups.

Green Apple Dessert

Apples are an important ingredient in many winter desserts, such as apple pie, apple crisps and crumbles, and cakes and strudel. However, they also make delicious desserts in the warmer months. Impress your guests, or your family, on a hot summer's day with this traditional dessert.

- **4 large green apples, peeled, cored and grated**

- **½ cup walnuts or pecans, coarsely chopped**

- **½ tsp vanilla**

- **½ cup icing sugar**

- **½ cup whipping cream**

- **Juice of one lemon**

1. Toss grated apples with lemon juice (to prevent browning) and combine with chopped nuts.

2. Stir in icing sugar and vanilla.

3. Top with whipped cream.

Serves 4.

Pears Poached in White Wine

Poached pears in white wine is an elegant dessert favoured by many Ukrainians at Easter time. It can, of course, be enjoyed at any time of year.

- **4 firm ripe pears**
- **1½ cups white wine**
- **2 tbsp red currant jelly**
- **¾ cup sugar or honey**
- **2 tbsp lemon juice**
- **2 whole cloves**

1. Pare the pears, leaving the stems attached. Use a melon baller to remove the core from the blossom end. Set aside.

2. Combine remaining ingredients and add to a pot large enough to fit four standing pears. Bring to a boil over medium-low heat.

3. Add the pears, cover and simmer about 20 minutes, or until pears are tender. (Use a skewer to test.)

4. Remove pears and stand on a serving plate or in a bowl. Continue to boil the sauce over medium-high heat until it is thick and becomes syrupy.

5. Pour the syrup over the pears and thoroughly chill.

6. Garnish with sweetened whipped cream.

Serves 4.

Tip: Make sure to use a good wine for this recipe, one that you would enjoy drinking.

Pears in Custard (Ukrainian Style)

Like peaches, pears are best when they are picked ripe. If they are very green, they will never develop a juicy, sweet taste. This is why I always recommend planting a pear tree of your own. Most everyone has enough room, and it's a great experience to watch it grow.

When I was in Ukraine, I was really impressed with the large number of fruit trees in everybody's yards there—plums, apples, cherries, peaches, pears, apricots, walnuts, all in one yard. So it can be done!

In our backyard here in Vancouver, my parents had two plums, a peach tree, two apples, sour cherry, sweet cherry, a walnut tree and of course a pear tree. Yes, all on a 33-foot lot!

This delicious dessert is very easy to make anytime. In a pinch you could use canned pears, but fresh pears of course are the best.

- **2 cups water**
- **¼ cup sugar**
- **Juice of half a lemon**
- **6 pears, pared, halved and cored**
- **2 eggs**
- **3 tbsp sugar**
- **1 cup scalded milk, cooled to lukewarm**
- **1 tsp vanilla**

1. For the syrup, bring the sugar, water and lemon juice to a boil.
2. Cook the pears in the syrup until tender.
3. Remove the pears and place in a serving dish. Keep the syrup hot.
4. Beat the eggs. Stir in the sugar, then add the milk along with 1 cup of the boiling syrup.
5. Cook the custard in a double boiler over hot water until the custard coats a metal spoon.
6. Stir in the vanilla and pour the sauce over the pears.
7. Chill and garnish with a few fresh strawberries if desired.

Serves 6.

Cherries with Sweetened Sour Cream

This combination is as delicious as it is unusual. The amount of sugar will vary according to the sweetness of the cherries, and personal taste. Just make sure when you're tasting to leave some for your guests!

- **1 lb cherries, pitted (about 3 cups)**
- **1 cup sugar, or to taste**
- **3 cups sour cream**

1. Sprinkle cherries with sugar.
2. Mix thoroughly until sugar is dissolved.
3. Top with sour cream.

Serves 6.

Prune Puff

The process of drying plums to make prunes is thought to have originated thousands of years ago in the same region where European plums originated – the Caucasus, between the Black and Caspian Seas. From there, they spread throughout South Central and Western Europe and the Balkans. This Ukrainian dessert using dried plums (prunes) is as light as a cloud, but very rich in favour. It's wonderful on its own, or served with a hot custard sauce, or lemon sauce. It was my sister Leone's absolute favourite dessert growing up.

- **1 cup cooked pitted prunes**
- **1 tbsp lemon juice**
- **4 large eggs, separated**
- **¼ cup sugar**
- **Pinch salt**

1. Chop prunes until fine, or press through a sieve. Combine with lemon juice.

2. Beat egg whites until stiff.

3. Beat egg yolks until thick and light-coloured. Add sugar and salt gradually to the yolks and continue beating.

4. Combine prune pulp with the yolk mixture. Fold in whites.

5. Spoon mixture lightly into a buttered baking dish. Set this pan in a larger pan, and add enough hot water to reach halfway up the pan containing the prune mixture.

6. Bake at 350°F for 45 minutes, or until center is firm.

7. Serve hot, warm, or at room temperature.

Serves 6-8.

Summer Berry Dessert

Sugared fresh fruits as well as fruits with sour cream and whipped cream have always been very popular with Ukrainians. Desserts like this light and luscious berry cake make such a claim very easy to believe.

The best berries to use in this recipe are strawberries, raspberries and blueberries. Other fruits can also be used, such as thinly sliced plums, peaches, apricots, nectarines, pears, or apples. The best yoghurt to use is whole milk yoghurt, as it has a higher butterfat content and provides a richer and creamier texture for this luscious dessert.

- **4 cups flour**
- **1 cup sugar**
- **½ tsp baking soda**
- **1 cup butter, softened**
- **1 cup yoghurt**
- **1 large egg, beaten**

Topping:

- **2 lbs berries**
- **¼ cup flour**
- **1 cup sugar (or more to taste)**
- **Icing sugar for dusting**

1. Mix flour and baking soda.
2. Cream the butter and sugar until fluffy.
3. Add the egg and yoghurt, and mix thoroughly.
4. Press dough onto a generously buttered jelly roll pan (or similar). Press dough down with your palm to flatten.
5. Mix flour with berries or fruit.
6. Top dough with berries or fruit, and sprinkle with sugar.
7. Bake in a pre-heated 350°F oven for 40-45 minutes.
8. When cooled, dust with icing sugar and servie with ice cream.

Serves 8.

Kozak Kisses

This lovely, crunchy macaroon is very easy to make, and even easier to eat!

- **4 egg whites (at room temperature)**
- **1½ cups sugar**
- **1 tbsp lemon juice (strained)**
- **2 cups walnuts, finely chopped**
- **Candied cherries**

1. Put egg whites, sugar, and lemon juice into the top of a double boiler. Cook over medium heat, beating mixture with an electric beater for 5 minutes, or until the meringue holds its peaks and the sugar has dissolved.

2. Remove the mixture from the stove and add the walnuts.

3. Line a baking pan with parchment paper that has been well-greased.

4. Drop from a spoon in round mounds. Press a candied cherry into the center of each cookie.

5. Bake at 350°F until set and delicately browned, about 25 minutes.

Makes about 3 dozen.

Tip: Beating egg whites at room temperature will always get you more volume. For even more volume, beat the whites in a copper bowl that has been warmed with hot water.

Honey Cookies

Various pastries using honey are traditional at Ukrainian Christmas and New Year holiday celebrations. Ukrainian honey cookies (called medivnychky in Ukrainian) are one of the popular favorites. As with many baked goods made with honey, these delectable cookies are best made several days ahead so flavors can develop.

- **1 cup honey**
- **¾ cup sugar**
- **½ cup corn oil**
- **4 cups sifted flour, divided**
- **1 tsp cinnamon**
- **4 large eggs, beaten**
- **2 tsp baking soda**
- **½ tsp baking powder**
- **¼ tsp salt**
- **¾ cup walnuts, chopped (optional)**

1. Boil honey and sugar together.

2. Remove and while still hot stir in 2 cups of flour and mix well.

3. Cool mixture and add oil, eggs and remaining flour sifted with the other dry ingredients.

4. Add walnuts and mix thoroughly

5. Shape dough into walnut sized balls and arrange them apart on a greased cookie sheet. Flatten balls slightly.

6. Bake at 325°F for 15-20 minutes.

Makes 7 dozen.

Old Country Honey Snaps

This cookie recipe is similar to ginger snaps and is very popular in Ukraine. These cookies have no fat, eggs or milk, so they are perfect for those who have to be careful about consuming fat or dairy products. They are fun to make and keep indefinitely – if well hidden.

- **2 cups buckwheat honey**
- **1½ cups sifted rye flour**
- **1½ cups sifted all-purpose flour**
- **2 tsp baking soda**
- **½ fresh lemon, zested**
- **1 tbsp whiskey or rum (or ½ tsp rum flavouring)**
- **½ tsp cinnamon**
- **½ tsp cloves**
- **½ tsp ground anise**
- **¼ tsp salt**

1. Heat honey to a boil and keep it hot.

2. Sift flours together and heat in a heavy frying pan, over low heat, stirring constantly just until hot. Be careful not to scorch.

3. Mix in the baking soda.

4. Add remaining ingredients to the hot honey and then stir in the hot flour. Beat until very thick.

5. Place the dough in a greased bowl.

6. Shape into walnut-sized balls. Place well apart on a greased baking sheet. Flatten with a fork.

7. Bake at 325°F for about 15 minutes until just golden. Do not brown or they will taste burnt.

8. Cool and let ripen for a day or two.

Makes about 2 dozen.

Sunflower Seed Crunchies

The rich, nutty flavour of sunflower seeds will burst in your mouth the minute you bite into one of these cookies! Sunflower is considered a national flower of Ukraine, while the seeds provide food for humans as well as birds. In addition to tasting wonderful, sunflower seeds are highly nutritious. They contain healthy unsaturated fats, protein and fiber, plus important nutrients like vitamin E, selenium, copper, zinc, folate, iron and phytochemicals. So enjoy the taste as well as the health benefits of this treat.

- **1 cup butter, softened**
- **1½ cups white sugar**
- **¾ cup golden brown sugar, packed**
- **2 large eggs**
- **1 tbsp vanilla**
- **1½ cups flour**
- **1 tsp salt**
- **1 tsp baking soda**
- **3 cups sunflower seeds, raw**

1. Cream butter and sugars until light and fluffy.
2. Beat in eggs and vanilla.
3. Combine flour, salt and baking soda, and add to sugar and egg mixture.
4. Stir in the sunflower seeds.
5. With floured hands, form 3 rolls about 2 inches wide.
6. Wrap in plastic or wax paper and chill.
7. Cut dough ½ inch wide and place 6 inches apart on a parchment-lined cooked sheet.
8. Bake in a preheated 350°F oven for 15-17 minutes. (Dough cold from the refrigerator will take the full 17 minutes.)
9. Rest a few minutes before removing from parchment paper.

Makes about 5 dozen.

Poppy Seed Cookies

Poppy seeds have always been important in Ukrainian cuisine and were found in most Ukrainian gardens. My mom and dad were the only ones in the neighbourhood who grew their own poppies, and I remember how beautiful the red flowers were.

I also remember how upset Mom was when we were notified by city authorities that we were no longer allowed to grow poppies—in our own yard! Later I learned that it was because at that time all poppy flower seeds contained opium, an illegal substance. But my, how times have changed. And it's nice to see poppies blooming in city gardens again.

- **1 cup butter, softened**
- **1 cup sugar**
- **2 large eggs, well beaten**
- **2 tbsp sour cream**
- **2¾ cups sifted flour**
- **¼ tsp baking soda**
- **½ cup poppy seed**
- **Pinch of salt**

1. Cream the butter and sugar until light and fluffy.
2. Mix in the eggs and sour cream.
3. Sift the flour with the baking soda and salt, then add the poppy seeds.
4. Mix the dry ingredients with the creamed butter and sugar.
5. Chill the dough thoroughly before rolling, for easy handling to about ¼ inch and cut with a floured cookie cutter.
6. Place on a greased cookie sheet and bake in a 375°F oven for about 12 to 15 minutes, or until golden or delicately browned.

Makes about 1½ dozen.

Tip: Remember to sift the flour before measuring.

Oatmeal & Sunflower Seed Cookies

Sunflowers have always been widely grown in Ukraine and today are a major export crop. Sunflower oil, especially the unrefined, cold-press variety, has a delightful flavour as well as being low in polysaturated fat.

Sunflower seeds add a slightly nutty flavour to this oatmeal cookie, a Ukrainian-Canadian hybrid. For even more sunflower flavour, replace half the butter with cold-pressed (unrefined) sunflower oil.

- **1 cup butter, room temperature**
- **1 cup brown sugar, firmly packed**
- **1 cup granulated sugar**
- **2 large eggs**
- **1 tsp vanilla**
- **1½ cups flour**
- **1 tsp salt**
- **1 tsp baking soda**
- **3 cups quick cooking rolled oats**
- **1 cup sunflower seeds**
- **1 cup golden raisins (optional)**

1. Cream butter and sugars until very smooth.

2. Add eggs and vanilla and beat well.

3. Add dry ingredients with the sunflower seeds and raisins. Mix thoroughly.

4. Roll into logs 2 inches in diameter. Wrap and chill thoroughly until firm. about 30 minutes.

5. Cut into ½ inch slices. Place on a parchment-lined cookie sheet.

6. Bake at 350°F for 18 to 20 minutes or until golden. Cool on racks.

Makes 5 dozen.

Carpathian Cookies

The meringue makes these cookies look like little mountain tops. They always bring back fond memories of my visit to Ukraine's breathtaking Carpathian mountains.

- **1 cup sifted flour**
- **½ tsp baking powder**
- **¼ tsp salt**
- **½ cup butter, softened**
- **3 egg yolks**
- **1 tbsp whole milk or cream**
- **3 egg whites**
- **1¼ cups icing sugar**
- **1½ cups finely chopped walnuts**
- **1 cup shredded coconut**

1. Sift dry ingredients.
2. Cream the butter until fluffy.
3. Add in the egg yolks, one at a time, and continue beating.
4. Stir in the milk or cream. Add the dry ingredients and mix thoroughly.
5. Chill for about ½ hour for easy handling.
6. Roll thin and cut into small rounds.
7. Prepare the meringue topping. Beat the egg whites until stiff. Add the sugar gradually, beating constantly. Fold in the walnuts and coconut.
8. Place the rounds in a greased baking sheet and top each with the meringue.
9. Bake at 350°F for about 12 minutes, or until delicately browned.

Makes 3 dozen.

Walnut & Honey Cookies

Ukrainians had an extensive bee culture from the earliest of times, when sugar was not known. As a result, Ukrainians have a lot of recipes for cakes, cookies, and other pastries that use honey. This recipe for walnut and honey cookies is a good example.

Be sure to allow these to ripen for a few days before you devour them. This is important. And remember, honey bees are the only insect that produce food for humans!

- **1 cup butter**
- **1 cup brown sugar**
- **1 cup liquid honey**
- **1 egg, slightly beaten**
- **4 cups flour, sifted**
- **½ tsp baking soda**
- **1 tsp cinnamon**
- **Pinch of salt**
- **1½-2 cups walnuts, chopped**

1. Cream the butter and sugar until light and fluffy. Stir in the honey and egg.

2. Sift the flour with the other dry ingredients and mix into the honey mixture.

3. Add the nuts. Mix well.

4. Drop from a teaspoon onto a greased or parchment-lined baking sheet.

5. Put the sheet on the middle rack and bake at 350°F for about 15 minutes.

6. Watch so as not to burn. Remember, all ovens are different!

7. Cool and store in an airtight container.

Makes 18-30 cookies.

Honey Prune Loaf

Prunes are actually the dried version of European (Italian) plums. They are a good source of vitamin A (in the form of beta-carotene), vitamins B and C, potassium, calcium, magnesium, iron and dietary fiber.

Unfortunately for the delicious and quite beneficial prune, its name has acquired a somewhat negative connotation, being associated with wrinkles, old age and sluggish gastrointestinal tracts. To help improve its image in North America, and for the benefit of those who might otherwise overlook its goodness in taste as well as nutrition, the prune is being re-labelled as "dried plum."

Whatever you call them, they are delicious, especially in this delectable loaf.

- **2 tbsp shortening**
- **3 tbsp sugar**
- **⅓ cup honey**
- **2 large eggs**
- **1 cup sifted flour**
- **⅔ cup whole wheat flour**
- **1½ tsp baking powder**
- **½ tsp salt**
- **½ tsp baking soda**
- **½ cup sour milk**
- **½ cup prunes, chopped**
- **⅔ cup walnuts, chopped**
- **1 tbsp orange zest**

1. Cream shortening, sugar and honey until light and fluffy.
2. Beat in eggs, one at a time.
3. Sift together flour, whole wheat flour, baking powder, salt and soda.
4. Add dry ingredients and sour milk alternately to the creamed mixture and blend.
5. Stir in prunes, nuts and zest.
6. Pour into greased 9x5x2 inch loaf pan.
7. Bake at 350°F for 1 hour or until cake tester comes out clean when inserted into the loaf.

Makes 1 loaf.

Honey Cornmeal Loaf

Honey is abundant in Ukraine and has been used for centuries in Ukrainian baking. The darker the color the stronger the flavor – that's why buckwheat honey, which is very dark, is often preferred. Baking with honey is a good thing. When honey is an ingredient in both cakes and cookies, texture, flavor and keeping qualities are greatly increased.

- **1 cup flour**
- **1½ tsp baking powder**
- **½ tsp soda**
- **1 cup cornmeal**
- **⅓ cup honey**
- **½ cup oil**
- **2 large eggs**
- **1 cup buttermilk**

1. Sift dry ingredients. Mix in cornmeal.

2. Cream oil with honey and eggs till fluffy. Mix in buttermilk.

3. Combine liquid with dry ingredients, mixing thoroughly.

4. Bake in a well-greased loaf pan at 400°F for 30-35 minutes, or until a tester comes out clean when placed in centre of the loaf.

Makes 1 loaf.

Lemon Caraway Seed Loaf

Caraway seeds aren't actually seeds, but the small fruit of the caraway plant. They have been used by East European cooks for centuries. In fact, caraway seeds are considered to have been used longer than any other spice in Europe; caraway has been found in neolithic villages dating as far back as 5000 years ago.

This small, crescent-shaped "seed" has a distinctive, pleasant flavour with a sweet undertone, which lends itself nicely to sweets like this lovely loaf.

- ¾ cup butter
- 1½ cups sugar
- 3 large eggs, separated
- 3 cups flour
- 1 tbsp baking powder
- ¼ tsp salt
- 1 tbsp caraway seed
- 1 cup milk

Lemon Glaze:
- 1½ cups icing sugar, sifted
- 3 tbsp lemon juice, or enough to make it spreadable

1. Cream butter and sugar until light and fluffy.
2. Add yolks one at a time.
3. Sift dry ingredients.
4. Alternately add dry ingredients with milk.
5. Add caraway seeds and fold in well-beaten egg whites.
6. Pour batter into well-greased 9x5x2-inch greased and floured loaf pan.
7. Bake at 350°F for 50 to 60 minutes, or until a cake tester comes out clean when inserted into the cake. Let cool on a rack.
8. Make lemon glaze by blending icing sugar in the lemon juice until smooth. Spread on cooled loaf.

Makes 1 loaf.

Apple Strudel

No one knows how strudel originated and no country can justly claim its origins. Regardless of its origins, however, it is definitely a favourite in central and eastern Europe, especially Ukraine. Today's cook is fortunate to have a fast and easy alternative to the time-consuming traditional strudel dough – a commercial product called phyllo pastry. It can be found frozen in most supermarkets and is a great time-saver that allows busy cooks to wow guests with this wonderful old-world recipe. Use this traditional Ukrainian apple and nut fruit filling, or any filling of your choice.

- **1 cup golden raisins**
- **2 cups chopped walnuts**
- **1 large tart apple, grated**
- **1½ cups sugar**
- **1 tsp cinnamon**
- **1 tsp lemon zest**
- **½ cup melted butter**
- **6 sheets phyllo pastry, thawed**
- **Fine dry bread crumbs**

1. Mix fruit, nuts, cinnamon, sugar and zest to make the filling.

2. Brush each sheet with melted butter and a sprinkling of bread crumbs, to make a stack of 6.

3. Place filling in a strip about two inches wide, two inches from the edge of the dough nearest you.

4. Roll like a jelly roll, turning the edges in as you roll it up. Brush the top with melted butter.

5. Bake at 350°F on a parchment-lined baking tray for 25 minutes, or until golden brown.

6. Rest for 15 minutes or more before serving. Serve with a dollop of whipped cream.

Makes 1 strudel (about 8 servings).

Tip: Thaw the phyllo in the fridge, to keep the sheets from sticking together. Rest for 1 hour on counter to bring to room temperature.

Poppy Seed Strudel

Poppy seed strudel is as popular with Ukrainians as poppy seed roll and is extremely easy to make using phyllo pastry. Some European delis even sell the filling, imported from Poland, which is excellent.

- **2 sheets phyllo pastry, thawed**
- **¼ cup butter, melted**
- **Fine dry bread crumbs**
- **2 cups poppy seeds, ground**
- **½ cup sugar**
- **½ cup golden raisins**
- **1 tsp lemon zest**

1. Mix poppy seeds, sugar, raisins and lemon zest.

2. Place one phyllo sheet on work surface with parchment paper. Lightly brush the sheet with melted butter and sprinkle with breadcrumbs.

3. Place the second phyllo sheet directly over the first, brush with butter, and sprinkle with breadcrumbs.

4. Spread poppy seed mixture on the long side edge of the pastry, and roll up gently, jelly roll fashion. Make sure to fold over a 2-inch edge at each end.

5. Place the parchment paper with strudel on a baking sheet.

6. Score individual portions with a very sharp knife.

7. Brush the top with melted butter.

8. Bake in a preheated 375°F oven for 25 minutes, or until crisp and golden.

Makes 1 strudel (about 8 servings).

Apple Dumplings

These delectable morsels are ideal as a chilled fruit soup garnish, as well as a light dessert.

- **2 tart apples, peeled and grated**
- **¼ cup sugar**
- **1 fresh lemon, juice and zest**
- **1 large egg, beaten**
- **¾ cup fine dry bread crumbs**
- **½ tsp ground cinnamon**

1. Mix all ingredients together.
2. Chill for 20 minutes.
3. Form into walnut sized balls.
4. Place in a pot of gently boiling salted water and cook until they rise to the top.
5. Remove with a slotted spoon onto a plate, keeping them separated, to avoid sticking.

Makes 8 dumplings.

Khrustyky

These crisp little dainties are light as feathers and seem to melt in your mouth almost immediately!

- **4 egg yolks**
- **2 tbsp sugar**
- **2 tbsp sour cream**
- **1 tbsp brandy or rum**
- **1½ cups flour**
- **Pinch of salt**
- **Icing sugar**

1. Beat egg yolks until light. Gradually beat in sugar.

2. Mix in other ingredients.

3. Knead on a floured board until smooth. Cover and let rest 10 minutes.

4. Roll very thin, about ⅛ inch thick. Cut dough into long strips about 1¼ inch" wide.

5. Then cut the strips into 2½ or 3 inch lengths crosswise or diagonally.

6. Slit each piece in the center and pull one end through to form a loose loop.

7. Fry, a few at a time, in deep hot fat (375°F) until delicately browned. Drain on paper towels.

8. Sprinkle with sifted icing sugar.

Makes 4 dozen.

Tip: Rum or brandy helps keep the dough from absorbing oil. But you need to use the real thing, not artificial flavouring.

Acknowledgments

As editor of this cookbook featuring the recipes of the late Sylvia Molnar, I would like to acknowledge and thank those who helped me along the journey to publication.

Sylvia's sister, Leone Retfalvi, for the inspiration to finish this project that was started so long ago. As well, Leone provided another set of eyes and caught so many "misses" in the copy that had slipped by both Sylvia and myself, even after we were sure we had caught them all! At times Leone and I both felt like Sylvia was in the room with us, peering over our shoulders. What a special delight.

The late Orysia Tracz, for cultural and historical clarifications and edits. I liked to call Orysia "a walking, talking Ukrainian encyclopedia," and certainly her encyclopedic knowledge of all things Ukrainian came through on the pages of this cookbook. Orysia passed away the year after Sylvia passed.

Loyal listener and dear friend David from New York, for all the encouragement (sometimes even prodding) to stick with it, and also for much needed, and appreciated, financial assistance.

Marsha Forchuk Skrypuch for her encouragement over the years, her mentorship, and for writing a foreword that moved me to tears.

Constance Diakow, Priscilla Gagnon and Myra Junyk for proofreading the final edit. Special thanks to Constance for connecting me with Katie Erickson.

Cheryl Andrichuk for proofreading the manuscript in the early stages of the project.

All my family, friends, listeners, colleagues, contributors, and supporters, who over the years have encouraged me to publish this cookbook, have patiently waited for it, and never gave up on me.

Katie Erickson, our project manager, for her professionalism and patience throughout the publication process, and for her kindness and generosity in sharing her expertise and feedback.

Management and staff at radio stations AM1470 CJVB Vancouver (1990-1996), AM1320 CHMB Vancouver (2000-present) and CHLY 101.7FM Nanaimo (2011-present), for bringing Nash Holos Ukrainian Roots Radio to the airwaves. Their ongoing support gave me the inspiration and the opportunity to broadcast Sylvia's recipes, cooking tips and personal stories on Ukrainian Food Flair, and to eventually compile them into this collection for print publication.

My husband Doug, for his broad shoulders, extraordinary patience and unwavering faith in me through all the ups and downs, setbacks and disappointments, triumphs and joys, on this journey.

Finally, Sylvia Molnar, whose humour, wit and professionalism set the standard for Ukrainian Food Flair on Nash Holos. She was an absolute delight to work with—utterly reliable and consistent, a stickler for detail, relentlessly cheerful, with a work ethic that left me in awe. And she never failed to make me laugh. May her memory be eternal, and may her spirit touch you through the pages of this collection of her beloved recipes.

Sylvia Pidraziuk Molnar

Sylvia fell in love with cooking even before she started school. Her mom regularly sent her to the neighbours to "cook" up a little storm for them. When she was allowed in the kitchen, she would perch on a special stool to reach the sink and stove. Other times she "cooked" in the living room, using the wood-burning fireplace as her "magic" stove, which earned her the nickname "Magic Cookie."

Born in Vancouver of Ukrainian parents who arrived in Canada during the second wave of Ukrainian immigration in the 1920s and 30s, Sylvia grew up in Point Grey steeped in Ukrainian culture. She graduated from the University of British Columbia in 1967 with a Bachelors of Education degree that launched her 26-year public school teaching career. She taught art and music but still managed to sneak in cooking lessons by including the cuisine of the country her students were studying. They made everything from cabbage rolls to sushi and moussaka!

Sylvia's absolute favourite hobby was creating new recipes based on traditional ones. Her recipes have been featured in The Vancouver Sun, St. Paul's Hospital Healthy Heart Newsletter, Bon Appetit magazine, the KCTS TV (Seattle) cookbook series and a Detroit Public TV cookbook.

In 1990, Sylvia became an independent teaching chef and consultant specializing in Mediterranean, Japanese, and central and eastern European cuisine. She cooked in diverse places, from TV sets and Ronald McDonald House to heritage kitchens in Vancouver's iconic Point Grey area.

In 1995, Sylvia opened Sylvia's Cooking School in Vancouver. Also that year, she began presenting Ukrainian Food Flair on the local Ukrainian radio program, Nash Holos.

Over the next several years, Sylvia conducted classes and demonstrations at the Granville Island Market Kitchen Cooking School, Cook School at The Cook Shop, Barbara Jo's Books to Cooks store, the Heart & Stroke Foundation, Cook Works on Broadway and The Bay Oakridge Market Square Cook School. She also did cooking demonstrations on Rogers Cable TV, Vancouver TV (now City TV), and KCTS TV Seattle.

Sylvia's cooking was inspired by her travels around the world, which she liked to call her "culinary tours." Her most cherished memories were of her two visits to Ukraine. The first was in 1968 where she found her maternal grandmother (Baba) in her mother's home village of Chernivtsi. She travelled alone by train from Budapest where she had been visiting her new in-laws with her husband who, having recently fled communism in Hungary, was persona non grata in the USSR. Her second trip was in 2003 during a much freer time on a guided tour where she discovered several more delicious Ukrainian recipes to share.

Sylvia passed away in 2015. She is survived by her sister Leone, who wanted this wonderful collection of recipes to be published as a tribute to Sylvia's memory and as a memento for Sylvia's friends, students, readers, viewers, and listeners.

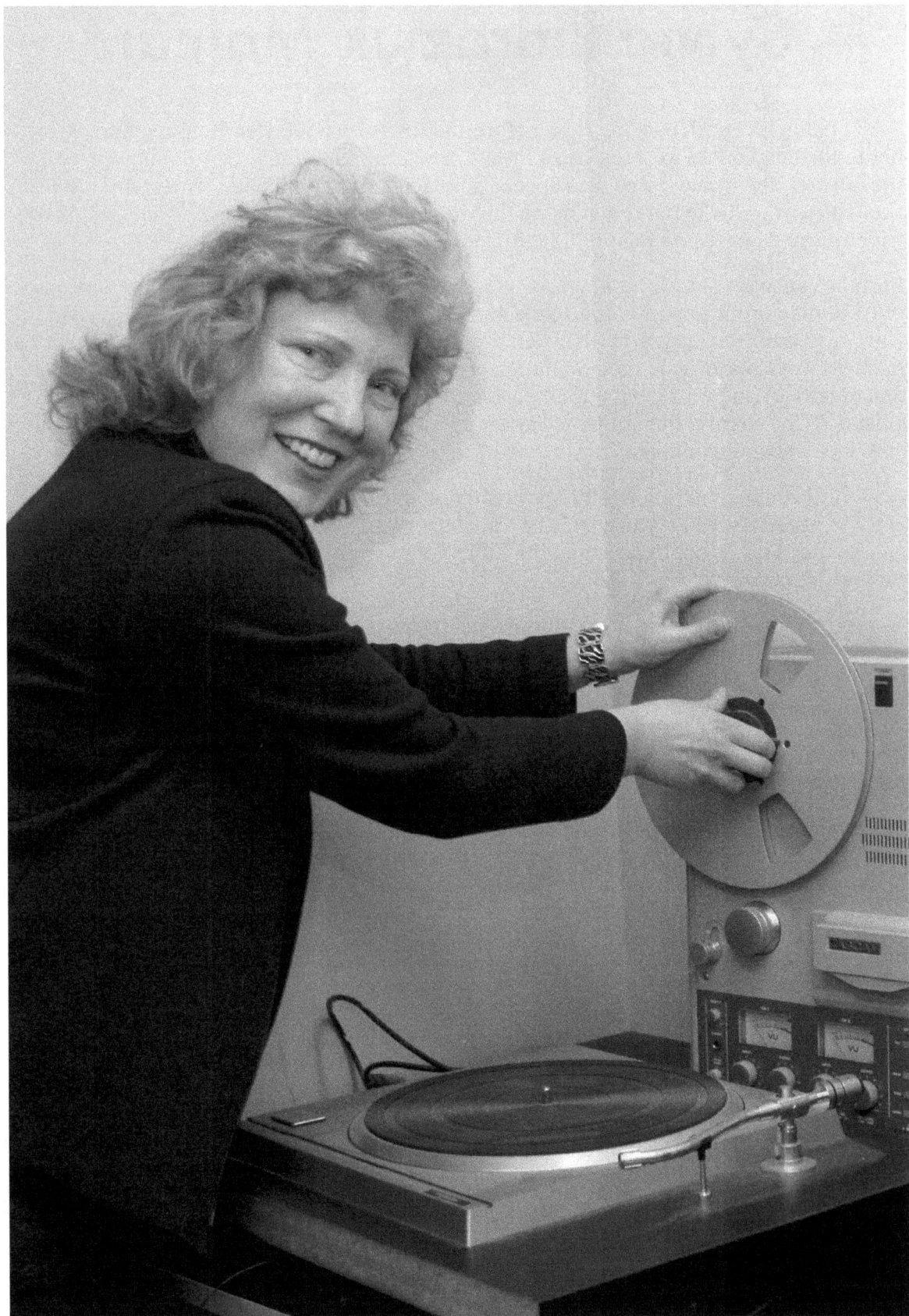

Paulette "Pawlina" Demchuk MacQuarrie

Paulette (aka Pawlina on Nash Holos) is descended from Ukrainian immigrants who arrived in Canada at the turn of the 20th century. All four grandparents emigrated from Halychyna (Galicia) and homesteaded in the Saskatchewan parkland area northeast of Regina. The childhood years she spent with her grandparents and living on the family homestead are among her fondest memories. In 1972, she graduated from Sacred Heart Academy in Yorkton, Saskatchewan, then moved to Winnipeg where she embarked on a career in the airline industry and eventually married.

In 1988, she moved to the west coast with her husband and soon connected with BC's Ukrainian community. In no time she found herself editing two community newsletters and co-hosting, along with Bohdan Zajcew and Eugene (Yevhen) Lupynis, a new Ukrainian radio program called Nash Holos ("Our Voice" in Ukrainian). The show ran on Vancouver radio station AM1470 CJVB from 1990-96, breaking the record for the longest-running Ukrainian radio program in BC's history going back to 1937.

In 1995, she made a career switch to freelance writing and editing. That same year it occurred to her that Sylvia Molnar, the food columnist for one of the newsletters she edited, might just add some spice to the radio show. Sylvia agreed, and the series "Ukrainian Food Flair" was launched on Nash Holos.

In 1996, Pawlina and her co-hosts disbanded, and the show went off the air. In 2000, she was approached by AM1320 CHMB to bring Nash Holos back to the Vancouver airwaves. Her former co-hosts gave her their blessing to revive the show on her own. The next year, she put Nash Holos on the internet, predating the term "podcast." In 2007, Nash Holos Ukrainian Roots Radio won the Roger Charest Sr. Award for Broadcast & Media Arts. That same year, the show broke its own record as BC's longest-running Ukrainian radio show. In 2016, the Nanaimo edition of the show won the NCRA Community Radio Award for Best Third Language Program.

In 2003, Sylvia resumed Ukrainian Food Flair, continuing to share her recipes, personal anecdotes and cooking tips with listeners for several more years. During that time, Pawlina and Sylvia tried unsuccessfully to self-publish a cookbook of Sylvia's recipes.

In 2010, Pawlina and her husband retired to Vancouver Island. The advances of technology in the broadcasting industry enabled her to continue producing the show remotely. That same year, the show began running in international syndication on shortwave, AM and FM to 20+ countries around the world with Taiwan-based PCJ Media for the next 10 years. In 2011, she syndicated Nash Holos on CHLY 101.7FM in Nanaimo.

In 2015, Pawlina was devastated to learn of Sylvia's untimely death. So it was a bittersweet pleasure for her to resume the cookbook project at the request of Sylvia's sister Leone. Going through all the original files again brought back happy memories that will now live on in the pages of this book.

Index

www.ingramcontent.com/pod-product-compliance
Lightning Source LLC
Chambersburg PA
CBHW062037090426
42740CB00016B/2934